THE LAY OF THE CID

An Epic of the
Spanish Reconquista

❖

ANONYMOUS

TRANS. BY R.S. ROSE & L. BACON

Lashed in the saddle, the Cid thundered out
To his last onset. With a strange disdain
The dead man looked on victory. In vain
Emir and Dervish strive against the rout.
In vain Morocco and Biserta shout,
For still before the dead man fall the slain.
Death rides for Captain of the Men of Spain,
And their dead truth shall slay the living doubt.

The soul of the great epic, like the chief,
Conquers in aftertime on fields unknown.
Men hear today the horn of Roland blown
To match the thunder of the guns of France,
And nations with a heritage of grief
Follow their dead victorious in Romance.

— The Lay of the Cid

cántaro
publications

www.cantaroinstitute.org

The Lay of the Cid (Cántaro Classics), Anonymous

Published by Cántaro Publications, a publishing imprint of Cántaro Institute, Jordan Station, ON. L0R 1S0, Canada

Book Design: Steven R. Martins

Library & Archives Canada
ISBN 978-1-990771-61-3

CONTENTS

FOREWORD

WITH THE PASSAGE of time, El Cid had become a legend. In Deborah Alcock's *The Spanish Brothers*, two young boys in sixteenth-century Spain recite a portion of the Spanish medieval epic, a faithful representation of how venerated and respected this *Campeador* came to be, this great knight of the *Reconquista*.[1] Several adaptations had been made of his life and mission, the most recent being the Amazon Original "The Cid". But how much is fact, how much is fiction, how much is embellishment, is unclear, save from what has been reported by the scholar Ramon Menendez Pidal (1869-1968), who, with his all his tools of scholarship and vigour of life, has rescued the historical Cid from being lost to fanciful fiction.[2] Numerous ballads, legends, and other tales have been written of El Cid. He remains to this day a universal hero to the Spanish,

1. Deborah Alcock, *The Spanish Brothers: A Tale of the Sixteenth-Century* (Jordan Station, ON.: Cantaro Publications), 16-17.

2. For more on the historicity of El Cid, see Ramon Menendez Pidal, *The Cid and his Spain*, trans. Harold Sunderland (London, UK.: F. Cass, 1971); Colin Smith, *The Making of the Poema de Mio Cid* (Cambridge and New York: Cambridge University Press, 1983); and Richard Fletcher, *The Quest for El Cid* (New York: Knopf, 1990).

though for how much longer we must ask considering the increasing liberal progressivism of European culture and its hostility towards anything Christian.

Yes, El Cid has been celebrated amongst Catholics and Protestants alike, and this is because of his role in the *Reconquista* – the recovery of Christian lands from occupying Islamic forces. In addition to capturing the wealthy Islamic kingdom of Valencia, for example, the Cid was also the first of the Christian leaders to defeat the *Almoravides*, a confederation of Muslim Berber tribes that had managed to establish an empire stretching from northwest Africa to Spain through their religious and militaristic zeal. Hispania was no foreigner to militant Islam; it was its victim. In the eighth century AD, immigrating Islamic forces established peace pacts and agreements with Spanish residents, what turned out to be the first strategic phase of the Islamic invasion. The second phase was when the peace pacts and agreements were nullified, a deceptive but justified practice according to *Shari'ah* (or Qur'anic) law. As the Islamic scholar Majid Khadduri writes:

> Islam, emerging in the seventh century... refused to recognize legal systems other than its own... willing to enter into temporary treaty relations with other states, pending consummation of its world mission. The Prophet and his successors, however, reserved the right to repudiate any treaty or arrangement which they considered as harmful to Islam...[3]

3. Majid Khadduri, *War and Peace in the Law of Islam* (Baltimore: Johns Hopkins University Press, 1955), vii, 202.

With the implementation of *Shari'ah* law, particularly that of the Maliki tradition, the Islamic forces had (i) burnt Catholic municipalities to the ground, (ii) flooded inhabited landscapes, (iii) destroyed vast treasuries of Christian literature, (iv) destroyed natural resources, and (v) demolished culturally significant buildings.[4] They razed everything to the ground to initiate a cultural "reset", from which they could build an Islamic culture – and this included renaming Hispanic regions with Arabic names (think of the term *Al-Andalus*). The *Reconquista* was a centuries-long series of battles by Christian kingdom-states to expel Islamic forces from Christian lands, it was a re-conquest, a reckoning, and El Cid played a pivotal role in that campaign. Historian Dario Fernandez-Morera comments on the *Reconquista* and El Cid's place in it:

> Spain's Christian armies were gaining strength. These forces were made up of hardy free peasant-soldiers and townspeople's militias from northern Spain, combined with a social class of noble knights born and bred for combat on heavy warhorses—the seemingly invincible Rodrigo Díaz

---

4. See Fernandez-Morera, *The Myth of the Andalusian Paradise* (Wilmington, DE.: Intercollegiate Studies Institute, 2016); and Soha Abboud-Haggar, *El Tratado Juridico de Al-Tafri de Ibn Al-Gallab: Manuscrito Aljaminado De Almonacid De La Sierra (Zaragoza): Edicion, Estudio, Glosario y Confrontacion Con El Original Arabe* (Zaragoza: Institucion Fernando el Catolico, 1999), 2:231.; and the English translation of *Mozarabic Chronicle* in Kenneth Baxter Wolf, *Conquerors and Chroniclers of Early Medieval Spain*, Second Edition ed. (Liverpool, UK.: Liverpool University Press, 2000).

de Vivar, "El Cid," was the most famous of these warriors.[5]

You might understand now the relevance of El Cid to the religious development of Hispania, and why he is considered a Christian hero in the face of Islamic oppression. What could have been if not for the *Reconquista*? What could have been without El Cid? But as with all men, El Cid had his own faults, and thus our view of him should be carefully tempered, bearing in mind the frailty of man's moral disposition and his perpetual need for a Saviour.

What you hold in your hands is the prestigious English translation of the *Cantar del mio Cid*, a poem written in the mid-twelfth century about the Castilian hero, Rodrigo Diaz de Bivar, relating to the events that took place from the time of his exile from Castile in 1081 to shortly before his death in 1099. This edition has been translated and edited by R. Selden Rose and Leonard Bacon. *The Lay of the Cid* explores the relationship of Rodrigo with King Alfonso VI of Leon-Castile. And as with many feudal epics, *The Lay of the Cid* portrays the breakdown of the vassal-lord relationship, generally due to the lord's shortcoming, and the vassal's attempt to resolve the situation, which in this case brings the reader to a climax and resolution in the form of a formal trial.

The Lay of the Cid is the second in our line of literary classics under the banner Cántaro Classics. If we wish to learn more about the Christian religious development of Spain and its colonial offspring, we would do well to ac-

---

5.   Dario Fernandez-Morera, Dario, *The Myth of the Andalusian Paradise* (Intercollegiate Studies Institute), Kindle Edition.

quaint ourselves with one of its most celebrated heroes of the *Reconquista*. Personally, I am drawn to its rich sense of honour, discipline, and courage, typical of feudal epics, and no doubt attractive to all men who aspire for manhood within the context of a Christian worldview. Here we have a man who commits himself to a greater authority (God and King), who is sacrificial and generous, determined, chivalrous, and committed to the truth. Here in this national epic we see not only El Cid the militaristic hero, but also the loyal subject, the man of faith, the loving family man, in truth aspects of his character that many do not see or care to pay enough attention to. Enough from my pen, however. All that I have left to say is that I commend *The Lay of the Cid* to your reading list, and to a special place on your bookshelves, where it deserves to be.

Steven R. Martins
Founding Director
Cántaro Institute, 2022

The Lay of the Cid is a translation of the *Cantar del mio Cid*, the national epic of Spain and a poem written in the mid-twelfth century about the Castilian Hero, Rodrigo Diaz de Bivar, relating events from his exile from Castile in 1081 until shortly before his death in 1099.

Translated into English Verse by R. Selden Rose
and Leonard Bacon

INTRODUCTION

THE IMPORTANCE of the Cid as Spain's bulwark against the Moors of the eleventh century is exceeded by his importance to his modern countrymen as the epitome of the noble and vigorous qualities that made Spain great. Menéndez y Pelayo has called him the symbol of Spanish nationality in virtue of the fact that in him there were united sobriety of intention and expression, simplicity at once noble and familiar, ingenuous and easy courtesy, imagination rather solid than brilliant, piety that was more active than contemplative, genuine and soberly restrained affections, deep conjugal devotion, a clear sense of justice, loyalty to his sovereign tempered by the courage to protest against injustice to himself, a strange and appealing confusion of the spirit of chivalry and plebeian rudeness, innate probity rich in vigorous and stern sincerity, and finally a vaguely sensible delicacy of affection that is the inheritance of strong men and clean blood.[1]

This is the epic Cid who in the last quarter of the eleventh century was banished by Alphonso VI of Castile, fought his way to the Mediterranean, stormed Valencia,

1. Cf. Menéndez y Pelayo, *Tratado de los romances viejos*, I, 315.

married his two daughters to the Heirs of Carrión and defended his fair name in parliament and in battle.

The poet either from ignorance or choice has disregarded the historical significance of the campaigns of the Cid. He fails to mention his defeat of the threatening horde of Almoravides at the very moment when their victory over Alphonso's Castilians at Zalaca had opened to them Spain's richest provinces, and turns the crowning achievement of the great warrior's life into the preliminary to a domestic event which he considered of greater importance. We are grateful to him for his lack of accuracy, for it illustrates how men thought about their heroes in that time. The twelfth century Castilians would have admitted that in battle the Cid was of less avail than their patron James, the son of Zebedee, but they would have added that after all the saint was a Galilean and not a Spaniard.

In order then to make the Cid not merely heroic but a national hero he must become the possessor of attributes of greatness beyond mere courage. The poet therefore, probably assuming that his hearers were well aware of the Cid's prowess in arms, devoted himself to a theme of more intimate appeal. The Cid, an exile from Castile and flouted by his enemies at home, must vindicate himself. The discomfiture of the Moor is not an end in itself but the means of vindication and, be it said, of support. When he is restored to favor, the marriage of his daughters to the Heirs of Carrión under Alphonso's auspices is the royal acknowledgment. The treachery of the heirs is the pretext for the Parliament of Toledo where the Cid shall appear in all the glory of triumphant vindication. The interest in the hecatombs of Moors and even in the fall of Valencia is a secondary one. What really matters is that the Cid's fair name be cleared of all stain of disloyalty and the doña Elvira and doña Sol wed worthy husbands.

This unity of plan is consistently preserved by a rearrangement of the true chronology of events and by the introduction of purely traditional episodes. The shifting of historical values may be due to the fact that when the poem was composed, about 1150, the power of the Moor had really been broken by the conquests of Ferdinand I, Alphonso VI, Alphonso VII and Alphonso VIII of Castile and alphonso I, the Battler, of Aragon. The menace was no longer felt with the keenness of an hundred years before, until the end of the tenth century the Moors had dominated the Peninsula. The growth of the Christian states from the heroic nucleus in northern Asturias was confined to the territory bordering the Bay of Biscay, Asturias, Santander, part of the province of Burgos, León, and Galicia. In the East other centers of resistance had sprung up in Navarre, Aragon and the County of Barcelona. At the beginning of the eleventh century the tide turned. The progress of the reconquest was due as much to the disruption of Moorish unity as to the greater aggressiveness and closer co-operation of the Christian kingdoms. The end of the Caliphate of Cordova was the signal for the rise of a great number of mutually independent Moorish states. Sixty years later there were no less than twenty-three of them. By the middle of the following century the enthusiasm that had followed the first successful blows struck against the Moor had waned, and with it the vividness of their historical significance and order.

Let us look at the Cid for a moment as he was seen by a Latin chronicler who confesses that the purpose of his modest narrative was merely to preserve the memory of the Cid of history.

When Ferdinand I of Castile died under the walls of Valencia in 1065 he divided his kingdom among his five children. To Sancho he left Castile, to Alphonso León, to García Galicia, to doña Urraca the city and lands of Zamora, and to doña Elvira Toro. Sancho, like his father, soon set about uniting the scattered inheritance. Ruy Diaz, a native of Bivar near Burgos, was his standard bearer against Alphonso at the battle of Volpéjar, aided him in the Galician campaign and was active at the siege of Zamora, where Sancho was treacherously slain. Alphonso, the despoiled lord of León, succeeded to the throne of Castile. Ruy Diaz, now called the Campeador (Champion) in honor of his victory over a knight of Navarre, was sent with a force of men to collect the annual taxes from the tributary Moorish kings of Andalusia. Mudafar of Granada, eager to throw off the yoke of Castile, marched against the Campeador and the loyal Motamid of Seville, and was routed at the battle of Cabra. García Ordoñez who was fighting in the ranks of Mudafar was taken prisoner. It was here probably that the Cid acquired that tuft of García's beard which he later produced with such convincing effect at Toledo. The Cid returned to Castile laden with booty and honors. The jealousy aroused by this exploit and by an equally successful raid against the region about Toledo caused the banishment of the Cid. From this time until his death he was ceaselessly occupied in warfare against the Moors.

The way to Valencia was beset with more and greater difficulties than those described in the poem. The events of the first years of exile are closely associated with the moorish state of Zaragoza. At the death of its sovereign Almoktadir bitter strife arose between his two sons, Almutamin in Zaragoza and Alfagib in Denia. The Cid and his followers cast their lot with the former, while Alfagib sought in vain to maintain the balance by allying himself with Sancho of Aragon and Berenguer of Barcelona. After a decisive victory in which Berenguer was taken prisoner Almutamin returned to Zaragoza with his champion, "honoring him above his own son, his realm and all his possessions, so that he seemed almost the lord of the kingdom." There the Cid continued to increase in wealth and fame at the expense of Sancho of Aragon and Alfagib until the death of Almutamin.

For a short time the Cid was restored to the good graces of Alphonso, but a misunderstanding during some joint military expedition brought a second decree of banishment. The Cid's possessions were confiscated and his wife and children cast into prison.

The Cid then went to the support of Alkaadir, king of Valencia. He defeated the threatening Almoravides flushed with their victory over the Castilians at Zalaca. Again he chastised Berenguer of Barcelona. he hastened to answer a second summons from Alphonso, this time to bear aid in operations in the region about Granada. Suspecting that Alphonso intended treachery, he withdrew from the camp toward Valencia. With Zaragoza as his base he laid waste the lands of Sancho and avenged himself upon Alphonso by ravaging Calahorra and Nájera.

Finally in 1092 the overthrow of Alkaadir prompted him to interfere definitely in the affairs of Valencia. He besieged the city closely and captured it in 1094. There he ruled, independent, until his death in 1099.

Even the Moorish chroniclers of the twelfth century pay their tribute to the memory of the Cid by the virulence of their hatred. Aben Bassam wrote:

The might of this tyrant was ever growing until its weight was felt upon the highest peaks and in the deepest valleys, and filled with terror both noble and commoner. I have heard men say that when his eagerness was greatest and his ambition highest he uttered these words, 'If one Rodrigo brought ruin upon this Peninsula, another Rodrigo shall reconquer it!' A saying that filled the hearts of the believers with fear and caused them to think that what they anxiously dreaded would speedily come to pass. This man, who was the lash and scourge of his time, was, because of his love of glory, his steadfastness of character and his heroic valor, one of the miracles of the Lord. Victory ever followed Rodrigo's banner – may Allay curse him – he triumphed over the princes of the unbelievers... and with a handful of men confounded and dispersed their numerous armies.[2]

One can hardly look for strict neutrality in the verdicts of Moorish historians, but between the one extreme of fanaticism that led Aben Bassam elsewhere to call the Cid a robber and a Galician dog and the other that four centuries later urged his canonization, the true believer can readily discern the figure of a warrior who was neither saint nor bandit.

The deeds of such a man naturally appealed to popular imagination, and it is not wonderful that there were substantial accretions that less than a hundred years later found their way into the Epic. Within an astonishingly short time the purely traditional elements of the marriage of the Cid's daughters and the Parliament at Toledo became its central theme. It is probable that such a vital change was not entirely due to conscious art in a poet whose distinguishing characteristic is his very unconsciousness. From his minute familiarity with the topography of the country about Medina and Gormaz, his affection for St. Stephen's, his utter lack of accuracy in his description of the siege of Valencia and from the disproportionate prominence given to such really insignificant episodes as the sieges of Castejón and Alcocer, Pidal has inferred that the unknown poet was himself a native of this region and that his story of the life of the Cid is

---

2. Aben Bassam, Tesoro (1109), cf. Dozy, *Recherches sur l'histoire politique et littéraire d'Espagne pendant le Moyen Age.* Leyden, 1849.

the product of local tradition.[3] Moreover there is abundant evidence to prove that before the composition of the poem as it has come down to us, the compelling figure of the Cid had inspired other chants of an heroic if not epic nature.

From this vigorous plant patriotic fervor and sympathetic imagination caused to spring a perennial growth of popular legends. The "General Chronicle of Alphonso the Wise," begun in 1270, reflects the national affection for the very chattels of the Cid. it relates that Babiéca passed the evening of his life in ease and luxury and that his seed flourished in the land.

After this constantly increasing biographical material had been developed and expanded through at least six chronicles and later epic treatment it was taken up by the ballads with a wealth of new episodes. Of these one of the most interesting is the Cid's duel with the conde Lozano and his marriage to Ximena. The hounds of Diego Lainez, the Cid's father, have seized a hare belonging to the conde Lozano, who considers that he has been grievously insulted thereby. Accordingly he retaliates with slurs that can removed only on the field of honor. Diego Lainez, too old to fight, in order to discover which one of his three sons is worthy of clearing the honor of the family, bites the finger of each one successively. The two eldest utter only cries of pain, but Rodrigo with great spirit threatens his father. He is chosen to fight the conde Lozano and slays him. Ximena demands justice for her father's

---

3. *Cid*, 1, 72-73.

death, and protection. Thereupon by order of King Ferdi-
nand the Cid and Ximena are married. Later we have Xi-
mena's complaints that her husband's activity in the field
against the Moors have tried her spirit sorely. There are
many ballads that treat of the arming and consecration of
the Cid in newly conquered Coimbra, of his victory over
five Moorish kings who gave him the name Cid (Master),
and became his tributaries, of the testament of Ferdinand
in virtue of which the Cid is made the adviser of Sancho
and Urraca. The siege of Zamora and the death of San-
cho are fertile topics. At the accession of Alphonso the
Cid forces him to swear a solemn oath that he was not
party to the murder of his brother Sancho. Finally when
the Cid is independent master of Valencia, the Sultan of
Persia, hearing of his exploits, sends him rich presents
and a magic balsam. This the Cid drinks when he is at the
point of death. It preserves his dead body with such per-
fect semblance of life that, mounted on Babiéca, he turns
the victory of the Moor Bucar into utter rout.

Not the least curious is the legend of the Jew who
having feared the living Cid, desired to pluck his sacred
beard as he lay in state in St. Peter's at Cardena. "This is
the body of the Cid," said he, "so praised of all, and men
say that while he lived none plucked his beard. I would
fain seize it and take it in my hand, for since he lies here
dead he shall not prevent this." The Jew stretched forth
his hand, but ere he touched that beard the Cid laid his
hand upon his sword Tizóna and drew it forth from its
scabbard a handsbreadth. When the Jew beheld this he

was struck with mighty fear, and backward he fell in a swoon for terror. Now this Jew was converted and ended his days in St. Peter's, a man of God.

The uninitiated reader will doubtless miss in the Epic more than one of his most fondly cherished episodes. If he prefer the Cid of romance and fable, let him turn to the ballads and the Chronicle of the Cid. If he would cling to the punctilious, gallant hidalgo of the early seventeenth century, let him turn to the Cid of Guillem de Castro, or to Corneille's paragon. Don Quixote wisely said:

> That there was a Cid there is no doubt,
> or Bernardo del Carpio either;
> but that they did the deeds men say they did,
> there is a doubt a-plenty.

In the heroic heart of the Epic Cid one finds the simple nobility that later centuries have obscured with adornment.

THE CID

CANTAR I

The Banishment of the Cid

I.

He turned and looked upon them, and he wept
    very sore
As he saw the yawning gateway and the hasps
    wrenched off the door,
And the pegs whereon no mantle nor coat of
    vair there hung.
There perched no moulting goshawk, and
    there no falcon swung.
My lord the Cid sighed deeply such grief was
    in his heart
And he spake well and wisely:
"Oh Thou, in Heaven that art
Our Father and our Master, now I give thanks
    to Thee.
Of their wickedness my foemen have done
    this thing to me."

II.

Then they shook out the bridle rein further
    to ride afar.

They had the crow on their right hand as they
    issued from Bivár;

And as they entered Burgos upon their left it
    sped.

And the Cid shrugged his shoulders, and the
    Cid shook his head:

"Good tidings, Alvar Fañez. We are banished
    from our weal,

But on a day with honor shall we come unto
    Castile."

III.

Roy Diaz entered Burgos with sixty pennons
    strong,

And forth to look upon him did the men and
    women throng.

And with their wives the townsmen at the
    windows stood hard by,

And they wept in lamentation, their grief was
    risen so high.

As with one mouth, together they spake with
    one accord:

"God, what a noble vassal, an he had a worthy
    lord."

IV.

Fain had they made him welcome, but none
    dared do the thing

For fear of Don Alfonso, and the fury of the
    King.
His mandate unto Burgos came ere the
    evening fell.
With utmost care they brought it, and it was
    sealed well
'That no man to Roy Diaz give shelter now,
    take heed
And if one give him shelter, let him know in
    very deed
He shall lose his whole possession, nay! the
    eyes within his head
Nor shall his soul and body be found in better
    stead.'

Great sorrow had the Christians, and from his
    face they hid.
Was none dared aught to utter unto my lord
    the Cid.

Then the Campeador departed unto his
    lodging straight.
But when he was come thither, they had
    locked and barred the gate.
In their fear of King Alfonso had they done
    even so.
An the Cid forced not his entrance, neither
    for weal nor woe
Durst they open it unto him. Loudly his men
    did call.

Nothing thereto in answer said the folk
    within the hall.
My lord the Cid spurred onward, to the
    doorway did he go.
He drew his foot from the stirrup, he smote
    the door one blow.
Yet the door would not open, for they had
    barred it fast.
But a maiden of nine summers came unto him
    at last:

"Campeador, in happy hour thou girdedst on
    the sword.
'This the King's will. Yestereven came the
    mandate of our lord.
With utmost care they brought it, and it was
    sealed with care:
None to ope to you or greet you for any cause
    shall dare.
And if we do, we forfeit houses and lands
    instead.
Nay we shall lose, moreover, the eyes within
    the head
And, Cid, with our misfortune, naught
    whatever dost thou gain.
But may God with all his power support thee
    in thy pain."

So spake the child and turned away. Unto her
    home went she.

That he lacked the King's favor now well the
    Cid might see.
He left the door; forth onward he spurred
    through Burgos town.
When he had reached Saint Mary's, then he
    got swiftly down
He fell upon his knee and prayed with a true
    heart indeed:
and when the prayer was over, he mounted on
    the steed.
North from the gate and over the Arlanzon he
    went.
Here in the sand by Burgos, the Cid let pitch
    his tent.
Roy Diaz, who in happy hour had girded on
    the brand,
Since none at home would greet him,
    encamped there on the sand.
With a good squadron, camping as if within
    the wood.
They will not let him in Burgos buy any kind
    of food.
Provender for a single day they dared not to
    him sell.

V.

Good Martin Antolínez in Burgos that did
    dwell
To the Cid and to his henchmen much wine
    and bread gave o'er,

That he bought not, but brought with him—
    of everything good store.

Content was the great Campeador, and his
    men were of good cheer.
Spake Martin Antolínez. His counsel you shall
    hear.
"In happy hour, Cid Campeador, most surely
    wast thou born.
Tonight here let us tarry, but let us flee at
    morn,
For someone will denounce me, that thy
    service I have done.
In the danger of Alfonso I certainly shall run.
Late or soon, if I 'scape with thee the King
    must seek me forth
For friendship's sake; if not, my wealth, a fig
    it is not worth.

VI.

Then said the Cid, who in good hour had
    girded on the steel:
"Oh Martin Antolínez, thou art a good lance
    and leal.
And if I live, hereafter I shall pay thee double
    rent,
But gone is all my silver, and all my gold is
    spent.
And well enough thou seest that I bring
    naught with me
And many things are needful for my good

company.

Since by favor I win nothing by might then
    must I gain.

I desire by thy counsel to get ready coffers
    twain.

With the sand let us fill them, to lift a burden
    sore,

And cover them with stamped leather with
    nails well studded o'er.

VII.

Ruddy shall be the leather, well gilded every
    nail.

In my behalf do thou hasten to Vidas and
    Raquél.

Since in Burgos they forbade me aught to
    purchase, and the King

Withdraws his favor, unto them my goods I
    cannot bring.

They are heavy, and I must pawn them for
    whatso'er is right.

That Christians may not see it, let them come
    for them by night.

May the Creator judge it and of all the Saints
    the choir.

I can no more, and I do it against my own
    desire."

VIII.

Martin stayed not. Through Burgos he
    hastened forth, and came

To the Castle. Vidas and Raquél, he demanded
    them by name.

IX.

Raquél and Vidas sate to count their goods
    and profits through,
When up came Antolínez, the prudent man
    and true.

"How now Raquél and Vidas, am I dear unto
    your heart,
I would speak close." They tarried not. All
    three they went apart.
"Give me, Raquél and Vidas, your hands for
    promise sure
That you will not betray me to Christian or to
    Moor.
I shall make you rich forever. You shall ne'er
    be needy more.
When to gather in the taxes went forth the
    Campeador,
Many rich goods he garnered, but he only
    kept the best.
Therefore this accusation against him was
    addressed.
And now two mighty coffers full of pure gold
    hath he.
Why he lost the King's favor a man may
    lightly see.
He has left his halls and houses, his meadow
    and his field,

And the chests he cannot bring you lest he
  should stand revealed.
The Campeador those coffers will deliver to
  your trust.
And do you lend unto him whatsoever may be
  just.
Do you take the chests and keep them, but
  swear a great oath here
That you will not look within them for the
  space of all this year."

The two took counsel:
"Something to our profit must inure
In all barter. He gained something in the
  country of the Moor
When he marched there, for many goods he
  brought with him away.
But he sleeps not unsuspected, who brings
  coined gold to pay.
Let the two of us together take now the
  coffers twain.
In some place let us put them where unseen
  they shall remain.

"What the lord Cid demandeth, we prithee let
  us hear,
And what will be our usury for the space of all
  this year?"

Said Martín Antolínez like a prudent man and
  true:

"Whatever you deem right and just the Cid
    desires of you.
He will ask little since his goods are left in a
    safe place.
But needy men on all sides beseech the Cid
    for grace.
For six hundred marks of money, the Cid is
    sore bested."

"We shall give them to him gladly," Raquél and
    Vidas said.
"'Tis night. The Cid is sorely pressed. So give
    the marks to us.
Answered Raquél and Vidas: "Men do not
    traffic thus.
But first they take their surety and thereafter
    give the fee."
Said Martin Antolínez:
"So be it as for me.
Come ye to the great Campeador for 'tis but
    just and fair
That we should help you with the chests, and
    put them in your care,
So that neither Moor nor Christian thereof
    shall hear the tale."

"Therewith are we right well content," said
    Vidas and Raquél,
"You shall have marks six hundred when we
    bring the chests again."

And Martin Antolínez rode forth swiftly with
    the twain.
And they were glad exceeding. O'er the bridge
    he did not go,
But through the stream, that never a
    Burgalese should know
Through him thereof. And now behold the
    Campeador his tent.
When they therein had entered to kiss his
    hands they bent.
My lord the Cid smiled on them and unto
    them said he:

"Ha, don Raquél and Vidas, you have forgotten
    me!
And now must I get hence away who am
    banished in disgrace,
For the king from me in anger hath turned
    away his face.
I deem that from my chattels you shall gain
    somewhat of worth.
And you shall lack for nothing while you dwell
    upon the earth.'

A-kissing of his hands forthwith Raquél and
    Vidas fell.
Good Martin Antolínez had made the bargain
    well,
That to him on the coffers marks six hundred
    they should lend.

And keep them safe, moreover, till the year
    had made an end.
For so their word was given and sworn to him
    again,
If they looked ere that within them, forsworn
    should be the twain,
The Cid would never give them one groat of
    usury.

Said Martin, "Let the chests be ta'en as swiftly
    as may be,
Take them, Raquél and Vidas, and keep them
    in your care.
And we shall even go with you that the money
    we may bear,
For ere the first cock croweth must my lord
    the Cid depart."

At the loading of the coffers you had seen
    great joy of heart.
For they could not heave the great chests up
    though they were stark and hale.
Dear was the minted metal to Vidas and
    Raquél;
And they would be rich forever till their two
    lives it were o'er

X.

The hand of my good lord the Cid, Raquél had
    kissed once more:
"Ha! Campeador, in happy hour thou girdedst

on the brand.
Forth from Castile thou goest to the men of a
    strange land.
Such is become thy fortune and great thy gain
    shall be
Ah Cid, I kiss thine hands again—but make a
    gift to me
Bring me a Moorish mantle splendidly
    wrought and red."
"So be it. It is granted," the Cid in answer
    said,
"If from abroad I bring it, well doth the
    matter stand;
If not, take it from the coffers I leave here in
    your hand."

And then Raquél and Vidas bore the two
    chests away.
With Martin Antolínez into Burgos entered
    they.
And with fitting care, and caution unto their
    dwelling sped.
And in the midmost of the hall a plaited quilt
    they spread.
And a milk-white cloth of linen thereon did
    they unfold.
Three hundred marks of silver before them
    Martin told.
And forthwith Martin took them, no whit the
    coins he weighed.

Then other marks three hundred in gold to
    him they paid.
Martin had five esquires. He loaded all and
    one.
You shall hear what said don Martin when all
    this gear was done:

"Ha! don Raquél and Vidas, ye have the coffers
    two.
    Well I deserve a guerdon, who obtained
    this prize for you."

XI.

Together Vidas and Raquél stepped forth
    apart thereon:
"Let us give him a fair present for our profit
    he has won.
Good Martin Antolínez in Burgos that dost
    dwell,
We would give thee a fair present for thou
    deserves well.
Therewith get breeches and a cloak and
    mantle rich and fine.
Thou hast earned it. For a present these
    thirty marks are thine.
For it is but just and honest, and, moreover,
    thou wilt stand
Our warrant in this bargain whereto we set
    our hand."

Don Martin thanked them duly and took the

marks again.

He yearned to leave the dwelling and well he
wished the twain.

He is gone out from Burgos. O'er the Arlanzon
he went.

And him who in good hour was born he found
within his tent.

The Cid arose and welcomed him, with arms
held wide apart:

"Thou art come, Antolínez, good vassal that
thou art!

May you live until the season when you reap
some gain of me."

"Here have I come, my Campeador, with as
good heed as might be.

Thou hast won marks six hundred, and thirty
more have I.

Ho! order that they strike the tents and let us
swiftly fly.

In San Pedro de Cardeñas let us hear the cock
ere day.

We shall see your prudent lady, but short shall
be our stay.

And it is needful for us from the kingdom
forth to wend,

For the season of our suffrance drawns
onward to its end."

XII.

They spake these words and straightaway the
    tent upgathered then,
My lord the Cid rode swiftly with all his host
    of men.
And forth unto Saint Mary's the horse's head
    turned he,
And with his right hand crossed himself:
    "God, I give thanks to thee
Heaven and Earth that rulest. And thy favor
    be my weal
Holy Saint Mary, for forthright must I now
    quit Castile.
For I look on the King with anger, and I know
    not if once more
I shall dwell there in my life-days. But may thy
    grace watch o'er
My parting, Blessed Virgin, and guard me
    night and day.
If thou do so and good fortune come once
    more in my way,
I will offer rich oblations at thine altar, and I
    swear
Most solemnly that I will chant a thousand
    masses there."

XIII.

And the lord Cid departed fondly as a good
    man may.
Forthwith they loosed the horses, and out

they spurred away.
Said good Martin Antolínez in Burgos that
    did dwell:
"I would see my lady gladly and advise my
    people well
What they shall do hereafter. It matters not to
    me
Though the King take all. Ere sunrise I shall
    come unto thee."

XIV.

Martin went back to Burgos but my lord the
    Cid spurred on
To San Pedro of Cardeñas as hard as horse
    could run,
With all his men about him who served him as
    is due.
And it was nigh to morning, and the cocks full
    oft they crew,
When at last my lord the Campeador unto San
    Pedro came.
God's Christian was the Abbot. Don Sancho
    was his name;
And he was saying matins at the breaking of
    the day.
With her five good dames in waiting Xiména
    there did pray.
They prayed unto Saint Peter and God they
    did implore:
"O thou who guidest all mankind, succor the

Campeador."

XV.

One knocked at the doorway, and they heard
    the tidings then.
God wot the Abbot Sancho was the happiest
    of men.
With the lights and with the candles to the
    court they ran forth right,
And him who in good hour was born they
    welcomed in delight.

"My lord Cid," quoth the Abbot, "Now God be
    praised of grace!
Do thou accept my welcome, since I see thee
    in this place."
And the Cid who in good hour was born,
    hereunto answered he:

"My thanks to thee, don Sancho, I am content
    with thee.
For myself and for my vassals provision will I
    make.
Since I depart to exile, these fifty marks now
    take.
If I may live my life-span, they shall be
    doubled you.
To the Abbey not a groatsworth of damage
    will I do.
For my lady do I give you an hundred marks
    again,

Herself, her dames and daughters for this
    year do you maintain.
I leave two daughters with you, but little girls
    they be.
In thine arms keep them kindly. I commend
    them here to thee.
Don Sancho do thou guard them, and of my
    wife take care.
If thou wantest yet and lackest for anything
    whate'er,
Look well to their provision, thee I conjure
    once more,
And for one mark that thou spendest the
    Abbey shall have four."
And with glad heart the Abbot his full assent
    made plain.
And lo! the Dame Xiména came with her
    daughters twain.
Each had her dame-in-waiting who the little
    maiden bore.
And Dame Xiména bent the knee before the
    Campeador.
And fain she was to kiss his hand, and, oh, she
    wept forlorn!

"A boon! A boon! my Campeador. In a good
    hour wert thou born.
And because of wicked slanderers art thou
    banished from the land.

XVI.

"Oh Campeador fair-bearded, a favor at thy
    hand!

Behold I kneel before thee, and thy daughters
    are here with me,

That have seen of days not many, for children
    yet they be,

And these who are my ladies to serve my need
    that know.

Now well do I behold it, thou art about to go.

Now from thee our lives a season must sunder
    and remove,

But unto us give succor for sweet Saint Mary's
    love."

The Cid, the nobly bearded, reached down
    unto the twain,

And in his arms his daughters has lifted up
    again,

And to his heart he pressed them, so great his
    love was grown,

And his tears fell fast and bitter, and sorely
    did he moan:

"Xiména as mine own spirit I loved thee,
    gentle wife;

But o'er well dost thou behold it, we must
    sunder in our life.

I must flee and thou behind me here in the
    land must stay.

Please God and sweet Saint Mary that yet

upon a day
I shall give my girls in marriage with mine
    own hand rich and well,
And thereafter in good fortune be suffered
    yet to dwell,
May they grant me, wife, much honored, to
    serve thee then once more."

XVII.

A mighty feast they had prepared for the
    Great Campeador
The bells within San Pedro they clamor and
    they peal.
That my lord the Cid is banished men cry
    throughout Castile.
And some have left their houses, from their
    lands some fled away.
Of knights an hundred and fifteen were seen
    upon that day,
By the bridge across the Arlanzon together
    they came o'er.
One and all were they calling on the Cid
    Campeador.
And Martin Antolínez has joined him with
    their power.
They sought him in San Pedro, who was born
    in a good hour.

XVIII.

When that his host was growing, heard the
    great Cid of Bivár,

Swift he rode forth to meet them, for his
    fame would spread afar.
When they were come before him, he smiled
    on them again.
And one and all drew near him and to kiss his
    hand were fain.
My lord the Cid spake gladly: "Now to our God
    on high
I make my supplication that ere I come to die I
may repay your service that house and land
    has cost,
And return unto you double the possession
    that ye lost."

My lord the Cid was merry that so great his
    commons grew,
And they that were come to him they all were
    merry too.

Six days of grace are over, and there are left
    but three,
Three and no more. The Cid was warned upon
    his guard to be,
For the King said, if thereafter he should find
    him in the land,
Then neither gold nor silver should redeem
    him from his hand.
And now the day was over and night began to
    fall
His cavaliers unto him he summoned

one and all:

"Hearken, my noble gentlemen. And grieve
    not in your care.
Few goods are mine, yet I desire that each
    should have his share.
As good men ought, be prudent. When the
    cocks crow at day,
See that the steeds are saddled, nor tarry nor
    delay.
In San Pedro to say matins the Abbot good
    will be;
He will say mass in our behalf to the Holy
    Trinity.
And when the mass is over, from the abbey let
    us wend,
For the season of our sufferance draws
    onward to an end.
And it is sure, moreover, that we have far to
    go."
Since so the Cid had ordered, they must do
    even so.
Night passed, and came the morning. The
    second cock he crew;
Forthwith upon the horses the caparisons
    they threw.

And the bells are rung for matins with all the
    haste they may.
My lord Cid and his lady to church they went

their way.

On the steps Xiména cast herself, that stood
the shrine before,

And to God passionately she prayed to guard
the Campeador:

"Our Father who art in Heaven, such glory is
in Thee!

Thou madest firmament and earth, on the
third day the sea.

The stars and moon Thou madest, and the
great sun to warm.

In the womb of Mary Mother, Thou tookest
human form.

Thou didst appear in Bethlehem as was Thy
will and choice.

And in Thy praise and glory shepherds lifted
up their voice.

And thither to adore Thee from Arabia afar

Came forth the three kings, Caspar, Melchior
and Balthasar.

And gold and myrrh and frankincense they
proffered eagerly.

Thou didst spare the prophet Jonah when he
fell into the sea.

And Thou didst rescue Daniel from the lions
in the cave.

And, moreover, in Rome city Saint Sebastian
didst Thou save.

From the sinful lying witness Saint Susanna

didst Thou ward.

And years two and thirty didst Thou walk the
    Earth, our Lord,

Showing, the which all men take heed, Thy
    miracles divine.

Of the stone, bread Thou madest, and of the
    water, wine.

Thou didst raise up Saint Lazarus according
    to Thy will.

Thou didst let the Hebrews take Thee. On
    Calvary the hill,

In the place Golgotha by name, Thee, Lord,
    they crucified.

And the two thieves were with Thee, whom
    they hanged on either side,

One is in heaven, the other he came not
    thereunto.

A miracle most mighty on the cross there
    didst Thou do.

Blind was Longinus never had seen from his
    birth-year.

The side of our Lord Jesus he pierced it with
    the spear.

Forth the blood issued swiftly, and ran down
    the shaft apace.

It stained his hands. He raised them and put
    them to his face.

Forthwith his eyes were opened and in every
    way might see.

He is ransomed from destruction for he

straight believed on Thee.

From the sepulchre Thou rosest, and into Hell
 didst go,

According to Thy purpose, and its gates didst
 overthrow,

To bring forth the Holy Fathers. And King of
 Kings Thou art,

And of all the world the Father, and Thee with
 all my heart

Do I worship and acknowledge, and further I
 implore

That Saint Peter speed my prayer for the Cid
 Campeador,

That God keep his head from evil; and when
 this day we twain

Depart, then grant it to us that we meet in
 life again."

And now the prayer is over and the mass in its
 due course.

From church they came, and already were
 about to get to horse.

And the Cid clasped Xiména, but she, his
 hand she kissed.

Sore wept the Dame, in no way the deed to do
 she wist.

He turned unto his daughters and he looked
 upon the two:

"To the Spiritual Father, have I commended
 you.

We must depart. God knoweth when we shall
    meet again."
Weeping most sore—for never hast thou
    beheld such pain
As the nail from the flesh parteth, from each
    other did they part.

And Cid with all his vassals disposed himself
    to start,
And as he waited for them anew he turned his
    head,
Minaya Alvar Fañez then in good season said:

"Cid! Where is now thy courage? Upon a happy
    day
Wast thou born. Let us bethink us of the road
    and haste away.
A truce to this. Rejoicing out of these griefs
    shall grow.
The God who gave us spirits shall give us aid
    also."

Don Sancho the good Abbot, they charged
    him o'er again
To watch and ward Xiména and likewise her
    daughters twain,
And the ladies that were with them. That he
    shall have no lack
Of guerdon let the Abbot know. By this was he
    come back,
Then out spake Alvar Fañez: "Abbot, if it

betide

That men should come desirous in our
company to ride,

Bid them follow but be ready on a long road
to go

Through the sown and through the desert;
they may overtake us so."

They got them upon horseback, they let the
rein go slack.

The time drew near when on Castile they
needs must turn the back.

Spinaz de Can, it was the place where the Cid
did alight.

And a great throng of people welcomed him
there that night.

On the next day at morning, he got to horse
once more,

And forth unto his exile rode the true
Campeador.

To the left of San Estévan the good town did
he wheel.

He marched through Alcobiella the frontier
of Castile.

O'er the highway to Quinéa his course then
has he bent.

Hard by Navas de Palos o'er Duéro stream he
went.

All night at Figueruéla did my lord the Cid
abide.

And very many people welcomed him on every
    side.

XIX.

When it was night the Cid lay down. In a deep
    sleep he fell,
And to him in a vision came the angel Gabriel:

"Ride, Cid, most noble Campeador, for never
    yet did knight
Ride forth upon an hour whose aspect was so
    bright.
While thou shalt live good fortune shall be
    with thee and shine."
When he awoke, upon his face he made the
    holy sign.

XX.

He crossed himself, and unto God his soul
    commended then,
he was glad of the vision that had come into
    his ken
The next day at morning they began anew to
    wend.
Be it known their term of sufferance at the
    last has made an end.
In the mountains of Miédes the Cid encamped
    that night,
With the towers of Atiénza where the Moors
    reign on the right.

XXI.

'Twas not yet come to sunset, and lingered
    still the day.
My lord the Cid gave orders his henchmen to
    array.
Apart from the foot soldiers, and valiant men
    of war,
There were three hundred lances that each a
    pennon bore.

XXII.

"Feed all the horses early, so may our God you
    speed.
Let him eat who will; who will not, let him get
    upon the steed.

We shall pass the mountain ranges rough and
    of dreadful height.
The land of King Alfonso we can leave behind
    tonight.
And whosoe'er will seek us shall find us ready
    then."
By night the mountain ranges he traversed
    with his men.
Morn came. From the hills downward they
    were about to fare.

In a marvelous great forest the Cid bade halt
    them there,
And to feed the horses early; and he told
    them all aright

In what way he was desirous that they should
    march by night.
They all were faithful vassals and gave assent
    thereto;
The behests of their great captain it behooved
    them all to do.
Ere night, was every man of them unto the
    riding fit.
So did the Cid that no man might perchance
    get wind of it.
They marched all through the night-tide and
    rested not at all.
Near Henáres a town standeth that Castejón
    men call.
There the Cid went into ambush with the men
    of his array.

XXIII.

He couched there in the ambush till the
    breaking of the day.
This Minaya Alvar Fañez had counselled and
    had planned:

"Ha, Cid, in happy hour thou girdedst on the
    brand.
Thou with an hundred henchmen shalt abide
    to hold the rear.
Till we have drawn forth Castejón unto the
    bushment here.
But give me now two hundred men on a

harrying raid to ride.
We shall win much if thy fortune and our God
    be on our side.

"Well didst thou speak, Minaya," the
    Campeador he said,
"Do thou with the two hundred ride on a
    harrying raid.
With Alvar Salvadórez, Alvar Alvarez shall
    advance,
likewise Galínd Garcíaz, who is a gallant
    lance.
Let them ride beside Minaya, each valiant
    cavalier.
Let them ride unfearing forward and turn
    from naught for fear.
Out unto Guadalajára, from Hita far and wide,
To Alcalá the city forth let the harriers ride.
That they bring all the booty let them be very
    sure,
Let them leave naught behind them for terror
    of the Moor.
Here with an hundred lances in the rear will I
    remain,
And capture Castejón good store of provender
    to gain.
If thou come in any danger as thou ridest on
    the raid,
Send swiftly hither, and all Spain shall say
    how I gave aid."

Now all the men were chosen who on the raid
    should ride,
And those who in the rearguard with the lord
    Cid should abide.

And now the dawn was breaking and morning
    coming on,
And the sun rising. Very God! how beautifully
    it shone!
All men arose in Castejón, and wide they
    threw the gates;
And forth they went to oversee their
    farmlands and estates.
All were gone forth, and the gates stand open
    as they were thrown,
And but a little remnant were left in Castejón.
Round the city were the people scattered the
    whole country o'er.
Then forth out of the ambush issued the
    Campeador.
And without fail round Castejón he rushed
    along his way.
The Moors, both men and women, he took
    them for a prey,
And of their flocks as many as thereabouts
    there strayed.
My lord Cid don Rodrigo straight for the
    gateway made,
And they that held it, when they saw that
    swift attack begin,

Fled in great fear, and through the gates Roy
    Diaz entered in
With the sword naked in his hand; and fifteen
    Moors he slew
Whom he ran down. In Castejón much gold,
    and silver too,
He captured. Then unto him his knights the
    booty brought.
To my lord Cid they bore it. The spoil they
    valued naught.

Lo! the two hundred men and three to
    plunder that rode out,
Sped fearlessly, and ravaged the country
    roundabout.
For the banner of Minaya unto Alcalá did
    gleam.
Then they bore home the booty up the
    Henáres stream
Past Guadalajára. Booty exceeding great they
    bore
Of sheep and kine and vesture and of other
    wealth good store.
Straightway returned Minaya. None dared the
    rear attack.
With the treasure they had taken his company
    turned back.
Lo, they wore come to Castejón, where the
    Campeador abode.
He left the hold well guarded. Out from the

place he rode.
With all his men about him to meet them did
    he come,
And with arms wide asunder welcomed
    Minaya home:

"Thou art come, Alvar Fañez, good lance thou
    art indeed.
Whereso I send thee, in such wise I well may
    hope to speed.
Put straightway all together the spoil both
    shine and mine;
The fifth part of all, Minaya, an thou so
    desire, is thine."

XXIV.

"Much do I thank thee for it, illustrious
    Campeador.
With what thou giv'st me, the fifth part of all
    our spoils of war,
The King Alfonso of Castile full well content
    would be.
I renounce it in thy favor; and without a claim
    to thee.
But I swear to God who dwelleth in the high
    firmament,
That till upon my charger I gallop in content
Against the Moors, and till I wield both spear
    and brand again,
And till unto my elbow from the blade the

blood doth drain
Before the Cid illustrious, howe'er so small it
    be,
I will not take the value of a copper groat
    from thee.
When through me some mighty treasure thou
    hast at thy command.
I will take thy gift; till such a time, all else is
    in thine hand."

XXV.

They heaped the spoil together. Pondered the
    Cid my lord,
He who in happy hour had girded on the
    sword,
How tidings of his raiding to the King would
    come ere long,
And Alfonso soon would seek him with his
    host to do him wrong.
He bade his spoil-dividers make a division fair,
And furthermore in writing give to each man
    his share.
The fortune of each cavalier had sped
    exceeding well,
One hundred marks of silver to each of them
    there fell,
And each of the foot soldiers the half of that
    obtained.
A round fifth of the treasure for my lord the
    Cid remained

But here he could not sell it, nor in gifts give
    it away.
No captives, men or women, he desired in his
    array.
And with the men of Castejón he spoke to this
    intent
To Hita and Guadalajára ambassadors he sent
To find how high the ransom of the fifth part
    they would rate.
Even as they assessed it, his profit would be
    great.
Three thousand marks of silver the Moors
    agreed to pay.
The Cid was pleased. And duly was it paid on
    the third day.

My lord the Cid determined with all his men
    of war
That there within the castle they would abide
    no more,
And that they would have held it, but that
    water sore it lacked:

"Ye Moors are friendly to the King; even so
    runs the pact,
With his host will he pursue us. And I desire
    to flee
From Castejón; Minaya and my men, so hark
    to me;

XXVI.

"Nor take it ill, mine utterance. For here we
    cannot stay.

The king will come to seek us, for he is not far
    away;

But to destroy the castle seems in no way
    good to me.

An hundred Moorish women in that place I
    will set free

And of the Moors an hundred. Since there, as
    it befell,

I captured them. Hereafter shall they all speak
    of me well.

Ye all are paid; among you is no man yet to
    pay.

Let us on the morrow morning prepare to
    ride away,

For against my lord Alfonso the strife I would
    not stir."

What the Cid said was pleasing to his every
    follower.

Rich men they all departed from the hold that
    they had ta'en

And the Moors both men and women blessed
    them o'er and o'er again.

Up the Henáres hastened they and hard they
    rode and strong.

They passed through the Alcárrias, and swift

they marched along,
By the Caverns of Anquíta they hastened on
    their way.
They crossed the stream. Into Taránz the
    great plain entered they,
And on down through that region as hard as
    they might fare.
Twixt Faríza and Cetína would the Cid seek
    shelter there.
And a great spoil he captured in the country
    as he went,
For the Moors had no inkling whatso'er of his
    intent.
On the next day marched onward the great
    Cid of Bivár,
And he went by Alháma, and down the vale
    afar.
And he passed Bubiérca and Atéca likewise
    passed,
And it was nigh to Alcocér that he would
    camp at last
Upon a rounded hillock that was both strong
    and high.
They could not rob him of water; the Jalón it
    flowed hard by.
My lord Cid don Rodrigo planned to storm
    Alcocér.

XXVII.
He pitched a strong encampment upon the

hillock there,
Some men were toward the mountains, some
    by the stream arrayed.
The gallant Cid, who in good hour had girded
    on the blade,
Bade his men near the water dig a trench
    about the height,
That no man might surprise them by day nor
    yet by night.
So might men know that there the Cid had
    taken up his stand.

XXVIII.

And thereupon the tidings went out through
    all that land,
How my lord Cid the Campeador had there
    got footing sure,
He is gone forth from the Christians, he is
    come unto the Moor,
In his presence no man dareth plough the
    farmlands as of yore.
Very merry with his vassals was the great
    Campeador.
And Alcocér the Castle wider tribute had he
    laid.

XXIX.

In Alcocér the burghers to the Cid their
    tribute paid
And all the dwellers in Terrér and Teca
    furthermore.

And the townsmen of Calatayúd, know well, it
    irked them sore.
Full fifteen weeks he tarried there, but the
    town yielded not.
And when he saw it forthwith the Cid devised
    a plot.
Save one left pitched behind him, he struck
    his every tent.
Then with his ensign lifted, down the Jalón he
    went,
With mail-shirts on and girded swords, as a
    wise man should him bear.
To draw forth to his ambush the men of
    Alcocér.
And when they saw it, name of God! How glad
    was everyone!
"The provender and fodder of my lord the Cid
    are gone.
If he leaves one tent behind him, the burden
    is not light
Of the others that he beareth. He 'scapes like
    one in flight.
Let us now fall upon him, great profit shall we
    gain.
We shall win a mighty booty before he shall
    be ta'en
By them who have their dwelling in the city of
    Terrér;
For if by chance they take him, in the spoil we
    shall not share.

The tribute that he levied, double he shall
    restore."

Forth from the town of Alcocér in wild haste
    did they pour.
When the Cid saw them well without he made
    as if he fled;
With his whole host in confusion down the
    Jalón he sped.

"The prize 'scapes," cried the townsmen.
    Forth rushed both great and small,
In the lust of conquest thinking of nothing
    else at all.
They left the gates unguarded, none watched
    them any more.
And then his face upon them turned the great
    Campeador,
He saw how twixt them and their hold there
    lay a mighty space;
He made them turn the standard. They
    spurred the steeds apace.
"Ho! cavaliers! Now swiftly let every man
    strike in,
By the Creator's favor this battle we shall
    win."
And there they gave them battle in the
    midmost of the mead.
Ah God! is the rejoicing on this morning great
    indeed.

The Cid and Alvar Fañez went spurring on
    ahead;
Know ye they had good horses that to their
    liking sped.
'Twixt the townsmen and the castle swiftly
    the way they broke.
And the Cid's henchmen merciless, came
    striking stroke on stroke,
In little space three hundred of the Moors
    they there have slain.
Loud was the shouting of the Moors in the
    ambush that were ta'en.
But the twain left them; on they rushed.
    Right for the hold they made
And at the gate they halted, each with a naked
    blade.
Then up came the Cid's henchmen for the foe
    were all in flight.
Know ye the Cid has taken Alcocér by such a
    sleight.

XXX.

Per Vermudóz came thither who the Cid's flag
    did bear.
On the high place of the city he lifted it in air.
Outspoke the Cid Roy Diaz. Born in good
    hour was he:
"To God in Heaven and all his saints great
    thanks and praises be.
We shall better now our lodging for cavalier

and steed."

XXXI.

Alvar Fañez and all ye my knights, now
    hearken and give heed
We have taken with the castle a booty
    manifold.
Dead are the Moors. Not many of the living I
    behold.
Surely we cannot sell them the women and
    the men;
And as for striking off their heads, we shall
    gain nothing then.
In the hold let us receive them, for we have
    the upper hand.
When we lodge within their dwellings, they
    shall do as we command."

XXXII.

The Cid with all his booty lieth in Alcocér.
He let the tent be sent for, that he left behind
    him there.
It irked the men of Teca, wroth in Terrér were
    they;
Know ye on all Calatayúd sorely the thing did
    weigh.
To the Sovereign of Valencia they sent the
    news apace:
How that the King Alfonso hath banished in
    disgrace
One whom men call my lord the Cid, Roy Diaz

of Bivár,

He came to lodge by Alcocér, and strong his
    lodgings are.

He drew them out to ambush; he has won the
    castle there.

"If thou aidest not needs must thou lose both
    Teca and Terrér,

Thou wilt have lost Calatayúd that cannot
    stand alone.

All things will go to ruin on the banks of the
    Jalón,

And round about Jilóca on the far bank
    furthermore."

When the King Tamín had heard it, his heart
    was troubled sore:

"Here do I see three Moorish kings. Let two
    without delay

With three thousand Moors and weapons for
    the fight ride there away;

Likewise they shall be aided by the men of the
    frontier.

See that ye take him living and bring him to
    me here.

He must pay for the realm's trespass till I be
    satisfied."

Three thousand Moors have mounted and
    fettled them to ride.

All they unto Segórbe have come to lodge

that night.

The next day they got ready to ride at
morning light.

In the evening unto Celfa they came the night
to spend.

And there they have determined for the
borderers to send.

Little enow they tarried; from every side they
came.

Then they went forth from Celfa (of Canál it
has its name),

Never a whit they rested, but marched the
livelong day.

And that night unto their lodging in
Calatayúd came they.

And they sent forth their heralds through the
length of all the land.

A great and sovran army they gathered to
their hand.

With the two Kings Fáriz and Gálve (these are
the names they bear).

They will besiege my noble lord the Cid in
Alcocér.

XXXIII.

They pitched the tents and got them to their
lodging there and then.

Strong grew their bands for thereabouts was
found great store of men.

Moreover all the outposts, which the Moors

set in array,
Marched ever hither and thither in armour
  night and day.
And many are the outposts, and great that
  host of war.
From the Cid's men, of water have they cut
  off all the store.
My lord the Cid's brave squadrons great lust
  to fight they had,
But he who in good hour was born firmly the
  thing forbade.
For full three weeks together they hemmed
  the city in.

XXXIV.

When three weeks were well nigh over and
  the fourth would soon begin,
My lord Cid and his henchmen agreed after
  this guise:

"They have cut us off from water; and our
  food must fail likewise.
They will not grant unto us that we depart by
  night,
And very great is their power for us to face
  and fight.
My knights what is your pleasure, now say,
  that we shall do?
Then first outspake Minaya the good knight
  and the true:

"Forth from Castile the noble unto this place
    we sped;
If with the Moors we fight not, they will not
    give us bread.
Here are a good six hundred and some few
    more beside.
In the name of the Creator let nothing else
    betide:
Let us smite on them tomorrow."

The Campeador said he:
"Minaya Alvar Fañez, thy speaking liketh me.
Thou hast done thyself much honor, as of
    great need thou must."

All the Moors, men and women, he bade them
    forth to thrust
That none his secret counsel might
    understand aright
And thereupon they armed them all through
    that day and night.
And the next day in the dawning when soon
    the sun should rise,
The Cid was armed and with him all the men
    of his emprise.
My lord the Cid spake to them even as you
    shall hear.

"Let all go forth, let no one here tarry in the
    rear,
Save only two foot soldiers the gates to watch

and shield.
They will capture this our castle, if we perish
    in the field;
But if we win, our fortunes shall grow both
    great and fair.
Per Vermudóz, my banner I bid thee now to
    bear;
As thou art very gallant, do thou keep it
    without stain.
But unless I so shall order thou shalt not loose
    the rein."

He kissed the Cid's hand. Forth he ran the
    battle-flag to take.
They oped the gates, and outward in a great
    rush did they break.
And all the outposts of the Moor beheld them
    coming on,
And back unto the army forthwith they got
    them gone.
What haste there was among the Moors! To
    arm they turned them back.
With the thunder of the war-drum the earth
    was like to crack.
There might you see Moors arming, that swift
    their ranks did close.
Above the Moorish battle two flags-in-chief
    arose,
But of their mingling pennons the number
    who shall name?

Now all the squadrons of the Moors marching
    right onward came,
That the Cid and all his henchmen they might
    capture out of hand.

"My gallant men here in this place see that ye
    firmly stand,
Let no man leave the war-ranks till mine
    order I declare."

Per Vermudóz, he found it too hard a thing to
    bear,
He spurred forth with the banner that in his
    hand he bore:

"May the Creator aid thee, thou true Cid
    Campeador,
Through the line of battle yonder thy
    standard I will take;
I shall see how you bring succor, who must for
    honor's sake."
Said the Campeador: "Of charity, go not to the
    attack."
For answer said Per Vermudóz: "Is naught
    shall hold me back."
Spurring the steed he hurled him through the
    strong line of the foes.
The serried Moors received him and smote
    him mighty blows,
To take from him the banner; yet they could
    not pierce his mail.

Said the Campeador: "Of charity go help him
    to prevail."

XXXV.

Before their breasts the war-shields there
    have they buckled strong,

The lances with the pennons they laid them
    low along,

And they have bowed their faces over the
    saddlebow,

And thereaway to strike them with brave
    hearts did they go.

He who in happy hour was born with a great
    voice did call:

"For the love of the Creator, smite them, my
    gallants ah.

I am Roy Diaz of Bivár, the Cid, the
    Campeador."

At the rank where was Per Vermudóz the
    mighty strokes they bore.

They are three hundred lances that each a
    pennon bear.

At one blow every man of them his Moor has
    slaughtered there,

And when they wheeled to charge anew as
    many more were slain.

XXXV.

You might see great clumps of lances lowered
    and raised again,

And many a shield of leather pierced and
    shattered by the stroke,
And many a coat of mail run through, its
    meshes all to-broke,
And many a white pennon come forth all red
    with blood,
And running without master full many a
    charger good.

Cried the Moors "Mahound!" The Christians
    shouted on Saint James of grace.
On the field Moors thirteen hundred were
    slain in little space.

XXXVII.

On his gilded selle how strongly fought the
    Cid, the splendid knight.
And Minaya Alvar Fañez who Zoríta held of
    right,
And brave Martin Antolínez that in Burgos
    did abide,
And likewise Muño Gustióz, the Cid's esquire
    tried!
So also Martin Gustióz who ruled
    Montemayór,
And by Alvar Salvadórez Alvar Alvarez made
    war
And Galínd Garcíaz the good knight that
    came from Aragon,
There too came Felez Múñoz the Cid his

brother's son.

As many as were gathered there straightway
  their succor bore,

And they sustained the standard and the Cid
  Campeador.

XXXVIII.

Of Minaya Alvar Fañez the charger they have
  slain

The gallant bands of Christians came to his
  aid amain.

His lance was split and straightway he set
  hand upon the glaive,

What though afoot, no whit the less he dealt
  the buffets brave.

The Cid, Roy Diaz of Castile, saw how the
  matter stood.

He hastened to a governor that rode a charger
  good.

With his right hand he smote him such a
  great stroke with the sword

That the waist he clave; the half of him he
  hurled unto the sward.

To Minaya Alvar Fañez forthwith he gave the
  steed.

"Right arm of mine, Minaya, now horse thee
  with all speed!

I shall have mighty succor from thee this very
  day.

The Moors leave not the battle; firm standeth

their array,
And surely it behooves us to storm their line
once more."

Sword in hand rode Minaya; on their host he
made great war,
Whom he overtook soever, even to death he
did.
He who was born in happy hour, Roy Diaz, my
lord Cid,
Thrice smote against King Fáriz. Twice did
the great strokes fail,
But the third found the quarry. And down his
shirt of mail
Streamed the red blood. To leave the field he
wheeled his horse away.
By that one stroke the foeman were
conquered in the fray.

XXXIX.

And Martin Antolínez a heavy stroke let drive
At Gálve. On his helmet the rubies did he rive;
The stroke went through the helmet for it
reached unto the flesh.
Be it known, he dared not tarry for the man to
strike afresh.
King Fáriz and King Gálve, but beaten men
are they.
What a great day for Christendom! On every
side away
Fled the Moors. My lord Cid's henchmen still

striking gave them chase.

Into Terrér came Fáriz, but the people of the
place

Would not receive King Gálve. As swiftly as he
might

Onward unto Calatayúd he hastened in his
flight.

And after him in full pursuit came on the
Campeador.

Till they came unto Calatayúd that chase they
gave not o'er.

XL.

Minaya Alvar Fañez hath a horse that gallops
well.

Of the Moors four and thirty that day before
him fell.

And all his arm was bloody, for 'tis a biting
sword;

And streaming from his elbow downward the
red blood poured.

Said Minaya: "Now am I content; well will the
rumor run

To Castile, for a pitched battle my lord the
Cid hath won."

Few Moors are left, so many have already
fallen dead,

For they who followed after slew them swiftly
as they fled.

He who was born in happy hour came with his

host once more.

On his noble battle-charger rode the great
    Campeador.

His coif was wrinkled. Name of God! but his
    great beard was fair.

His mail-hood on his shoulders lay. His sword
    in hand he bare.

And he looked upon his henchmen and saw
    them drawing nigh:

"Since we ha' won such a battle, glory to God
    on high!"

The Cid his henchmen plundered the
    encampment far and wide

Of the shields and of the weapons and other
    wealth beside.

Of the Moors they captured there were found
    five hundred steeds and ten.

And there was great rejoicing among those
    Christian men,

And the lost of their number were but fifteen
    all told.

They brought a countless treasure of silver
    and of gold.

Enriched were all those Christians with the
    spoil that they had ta'en

And back unto their castle they restored the
    Moors again;

To give them something further he gave

command and bade.
With all his train of henchmen the Cid was
passing glad.
He gave some monies, some much goods to be
divided fair,
And full an hundred horses fell to the Cid's
fifth share.
God's name! his every vassal nobly did he
requite,
Not only the foot soldiers but likewise every
knight.
He who in happy hour was born wrought well
his government,
And all whom he brought with him therewith
were well content.

"Harken to me, Minaya, my own right arm art
thou.
Of the wealth, wherewith our army the
Creator did endow,
Take in thine hand whatever thou deemest
good to choose.
To Castile I fain would send thee to carry
there the news
Of our triumph. To Alphonso the King who
banished me
A gift of thirty horses I desire to send with
thee.
Saddled is every charger, each steed is bridled
well.

There hangeth a good war-sword at the
    pommel of each selle."
Said Minaya Alvar Fañez: "I will do it with
    good cheer."

XLI.

"Of the gold and the fine silver, behold a
    bootful here.
Nothing thereto is lacking. Thou shalt pay the
    money down
At Saint Mary's Church for masses fifty score
    in Burgos town;
To my wife and to my daughters the
    remainder do thou bear.
Let them offer day and night for me
    continually their prayer.
If I live, exceeding wealthy all of those dames
    shall be."

XLII.

Minaya Alvar Fañez, therewith content was
    he.
They made a choice of henchmen along with
    him to ride.
They fed the steeds. Already came on the
    eventide.
Roy Diaz would decide it with his companions
    leal.

XLIII.

"Dost thou then go, Minaya, to the great land

of Castile
And unto our well-wishers with a clear heart
    canst thou say:
'God granted us his favor, and we conquered
    in the fray?'
If returning thou shalt find us here in this
    place, 'tis well;
If not, where thou shalt hear of us, go seek us
    where we dwell.
For we must gain our daily bread with the
    lance and with the brand,
Since otherwise we perish here in a barren
    land.
And therefore as methinketh, we must get
    hence away."

XLIV.

So was it, and Minaya went at the break of
    day.
But there behind the Campeador abode with
    all his band.
And waste was all the country, an exceeding
    barren land.
Each day upon my lord the Cid there in that
    place they spied,
The Moors that dwelt on the frontier and
    outlanders beside.
Healed was King Fáriz. With him they held a
    council there,
The folk that dwelt in Teca and the townsmen

of Terrér,

And the people of Calatayúd, of the three the
    fairest town.

In such wise have they valued it and on
    parchment set it down

That for silver marks three thousand Alcocér
    the Cid did sell.

XLV.

Roy Diaz sold them Alcocér. How excellently
    well

He paid his vassals! Horse and foot he made
    them wealthy then,

And a poor man you could not find in all his
    host of men.

In joy he dwelleth aye who serves a lord of
    noble heart.

XLVI.

When my lord the Cid was ready from the
    Castle to depart,

The Moors both men and women cried out in
    bitter woe:

"Lord Cid art thou departing? Still may our
    prayers go

Before thy path, for with thee we are full well
    content."

For my lord the great Cid of Bivár, when from
    Alcocér he went,

The Moors both men and women made
    lamentation sore.

He lifted up the standard, forth marched the
    Campeador.
Down the Jalón he hastened, on he went
    spurring fast.
He saw birds of happy omen, as from the
    stream he passed.
Glad were the townsmen of Terrér that he had
    marched away,
And the dwellers in Calatayúd were better
    pleased than they.
But in the town of Alcocér 'twas grief to all
    and one,
For many a deed of mercy unto them the Cid
    had done.
My lord the Cid spurred onward. Forward
    apace he went;
'Twas near to the hill Monreál that he let
    pitch his tent.
Great is the hill and wondrous and very high
    likewise.
Be it known from no quarter doth he need to
    dread surprise.
And first he forced Doróca tribute to him to
    pay,
And then levied on Molína on the other side
    that lay,
Teruél o'er against him to submit he next
    compelled
And lastly Celfa de Canál within his power he
    held.

XLVII.

May my lord the Cid, Roy Diaz, at all times
      God's favor feel.

Minaya Alvar Fañez has departed to Castile.

To the King thirty horses for a present did he
      bring.

And when he had beheld them beautifully
      smiled the King:

"Who gave thee these, Minaya, so prosper
      thee the Lord?"

"Even the Cid Roy Diaz, who in good hour
      girded sword.

Since you banished him, by cunning has he
      taken Alcocér.

To the King of Valencia the tidings did they
      bear.

He bade that they besiege him; from every
      water-well

They cut him off. He sallied forth from the
      citadel,

In the open field he fought them, and he beat
      in that affray

Two Moorish kings he captured, sire, a very
      mighty prey.

Great King, this gift he sends thee. Thine
      hands and feet also

He kisses. Show him mercy; such God to thee
      shall show."

Said the King:

"'Tis over early for one banished, without

grace

In his lord's sight, to receive it at the end of
    three week's space.

But since 'tis Moorish plunder to take it I
    consent.

That the Cid has taken such a spoil, I am full
    well content.

Beyond all this. Minaya. thine exemption I
    accord,

For all thy lands and honors are unto thee
    restored.

Go and come! Henceforth my favor I grant to
    thee once more.

But to thee I say nothing of the Cid
    Campeador.

XLVIII.

"Beyond this, Alvar Fañez, I am fain to tell it
    thee

That whosoever in my realm in that desire
    may be,

Let them, the brave and gallant, to the Cid
    betake them straight.

I free them and exempt them both body and
    estate."

Minaya Alvar Fañez has kissed the King's
    hands twain:

"Great thanks, as to my rightful lord I give
    thee, King, again.

This dost thou now, and better yet as at some

later hour.

We shall labor to deserve it, if God will give us
    power."

Said the King: "Minaya, peace for that. Take
    through Castile thy way.

None shall molest. My lord the Cid seek forth
    without delay."

XLIX.

Of him I fain would tell you in good hour that
    girt the blade.

The hill, where his encampment in that
    season he had made,

While the Moorish folk endureth, while there
    are Christians still,

Shall they ever name in writing 'My Lord the
    Cid, his Hill.'

While he was there great ravage in all the
    land he made,

Under tribute the whole valley of the Martin
    he laid.

And unto Zaragoza did the tidings of him go,

Nor pleased the Moors; nay rather they were
    filled with grievous woe.

For fifteen weeks together my lord Cid there
    did stay.

When the good knight saw how greatly
    Minaya did delay,

Then forth with all his henchmen on a night
    march he tried.

And he left all behind him, and forsook the
    mountain side,
Beyond the town of Teruél good don Rodrigo
    went.
In the pine grove of Tévar Roy Diaz pitched
    his tent.
And all the lands about him he harried in the
    raid,
And on Zaragoza city a heavy tribute laid.

When this he had accomplished and three
    weeks had made an end,
Out of Castile Minaya unto the Cid did wend.
Two hundred knights were with him that had
    belted on the brands.
Know ye well that there were many foot-
    soldiers in his bands.
When the Cid saw Minaya draw near unto his
    view,
With his horse at a full gallop to embrace the
    man he flew.
He kissed his mouth, his very eyes in that
    hour kissed the Cid.
And then all things he told him, for naught
    from him he hid.
Then beautifully upon him smiled the good
    Campeador:
"God and his righteousness divine be greatly
    praised therefor.
While thou shalt live, Minaya, well goeth this

my game."

L.

God! How happy was the army that thus
    Minaya came,
For of them they left behind them he brought
    the tidings in,
From comrade and from brethren and the
    foremost of their kin.

LI.

But God! What a glad aspect the Cid fair-
    bearded wore
That duly had Minaya paid for masses fifty
    score,
And of his wife and daughters all of the state
    displayed!
God! How content was he thereat! What noble
    cheer he made!

"Ha! Alvar Fañez, many now may thy life-days
    be.
What fair despatch thou madest! Thou art
    worth more than we."

LII.

And he who in good hour was born tarried in
    no way then,
But he took knights two hundred, and all
    were chosen men;
And forth when fell the evening a-raiding did
    they haste.

At Alcañiz the meadows the Campeador laid
    waste,
And gave all places round about to ravage and
    to sack.
On the third day to whence he came the Cid
    again turned back.

LIII.

Thro' all the country roundabout have the
    tidings of them flown.
It grieved the men of Huésca and the people
    of Monzón.
Glad were they in Zaragoza since the tribute
    they had paid,
For outrage at Roy Diaz's hand no whit were
    they afraid.

LIV.

Then back to their encampment they
    hastened with their prey.
All men were very merry for a mighty spoil
    had they.
The Cid was glad exceeding; Alvar Fañez liked
    it well.
But the great Cid smiled, for there at ease he
    could not bear to dwell.

"Ha! All my knights, unto you the truth will I
    confess:
Who still in one place tarries, his fortune will
    grow less.

Let us tomorrow morning prepare to ride
      apace,
Let us march and leave forever our
      encampment in this place."
Unto the pass of Alucát the lord Cid got him
      gone.
Then to Huésca and to Montalban he hastily
      marched on.
And ten full days together on that raid they
      were to ride.
The tidings to all quarters went flying far and
      wide,
how that the Exile from Castile great harm to
      them had done.

LV.

Afar into all quarters did the tidings of him
      run.
They brought the message to the Count of
      Barcelona's hand,
How that the Cid Roy Diaz was o'errunning all
      the land.
He was wroth. For a sore insult the tiding did
      he take.

LVI.

The Count was a great braggart and an empty
      word he spake:
"Great wrongs he put upon me, he of Bivár,
      the Cid.
Within my very palace much shame to me

he did:

He gave no satisfaction though he struck my
    brother's son;

And the lands in my keeping now doth he
    over-run.

I challenged him not; our pact of peace I did
    not overthrow;

But since he seeks it of me, to demand it I will
    go."

He gathered then his powers that were
    exceeding strong,

Great bands of Moors and Christians to his
    array did throng.

After the lord Cid of Bivár they went upon
    their way,

Three nights and days together upon the
    march were they.

At length in Tévar's pine grove the Cid they
    have o'erta'en.

So strong were they that captive to take him
    were they fain.

My lord Cid don Rodrigo bearing great spoil
    he went.

From the ridge unto the valley he had
    finished the descent.

And in that place they bore him Count don
    Remónd his word.

My lord Cid sent unto him when the message

he had heard:

"Say to the Count that it were well his anger
  now should cease.
No goods of his I carry. Let him leave me in
  peace."

Thereto the Count gave answer: "Not so the
  matter ends.
For what was and is of evil he shall make me
  full amends.
The Exile shall know swiftly whom he has
  sought to slight."

Back hastened the ambassador as swiftly as he
  might.
And then my lord Cid of Bivár knew how the
  matter lay,
And that without a battle they could not get
  away.

LVII.
"Ha! lay aside your booty now, every cavalier,
And take in hand your weapons, and get on
  your battle-gear.
Count don Remónd against us will deliver
  battle strong;
Great bands of Moors and Christians he
  brings with him along.
He will not for any reason without fighting
  let us go.

Here let us have the battle since they pursue
    us so.
So get you on your armour and girth the
    horses tight.
Down the hill they come in hosen and their
    saddles are but light,
And loose their girths. Each man of us has a
    Galician selle,
And moreover with the jackboots are our
    hosen covered well.
We should beat them though we numbered
    but five score cavaliers.
Before they reach the level, let us front them
    with the spears.
For each you strike three saddles thereby shall
    empty go.
Who was the man he hunted, Remónd
    Berenguél shall know
This day in Tévar's pine grove, who would
    take from me my prey."

LVIII.
When thus the Cid had spoken, were all in
    good array;
They had taken up their weapons and each
    had got to horse.
They beheld the Frankish army down the hill
    that held its course.
And at the end of the descent, close to the
    level land,

The Cid who in good hour was born, to charge
   them gave command.
And this did his good henchmen perform
   with all their heart;
With the pennons and the lances they nobly
   played their part,
Smiting at some, and others overthrowing in
   their might.
He who was born in happy hour has
   conquered in the fight.
There the Count don Remónd he took a
   prisoner of war,
And Coláda the war-falchion worth a
   thousand marks and more.

LIX.
By the victory there much honor unto his
   beard he did.
And then the Count to his own tent was taken
   by the Cid.
He bade his squires guard him. From the tent
   he hastened then.
From every side together about him came his
   men.
The Cid was glad, so mighty were the spoils of
   that defeat.
For the lord Cid don Rodrigo they prepared
   great stock of meat.
But namely the Count don Remónd, thereby
   he set no store.

To him they brought the viands, and placed
    them him before.
He would not eat, and at them all he mocked
    with might and main:

"I will not eat a mouthful for all the wealth in
    Spain;
Rather will I lose my body and forsake my soul
    forby,
Since beaten in the battle by such tattered
    louts was I."

LX.

My lord the Cid Roy Diaz you shall hearken
    what he said:
"Drink of the wine I prithee, Count, eat also
    of the bread.
If this thou dost, no longer shalt thou be a
    captive then;
If not, then shalt thou never see Christendom
    again."

LXI.

"Do thou eat, don Rodrigo, and prepare to
    slumber sweet.
For myself I will let perish, and nothing will I
    eat."
And in no way were they able to prevail till
    the third day,
Nor make him eat a mouthful while they
    portioned the great prey.

LXII.

"Ho! Count, do thou eat somewhat," even so
    my lord Cid spoke,
"If thou dost not eat, thou shalt not look
    again on Christian folk;
If in such guise thou eatest that my will is
    satisfied,
Thyself, Count, and, moreover, two noblemen
    beside
Will I make free of your persons and set at
    liberty."

And when the Count had heard it exceeding
    glad was he.
"Cid, if thou shalt perform it, this promise
    thou dost give,
Thereat I much shall marvel as long as I shall
    live."
"Eat then, oh Count; when fairly thy dinner
    thou hast ta'en
I will then set at liberty thee and the other
    twain.
But what in open battle thou didst lose and I
    did earn,
Know that not one poor farthing's worth to
    thee will I return,
For I need it for these henchmen who hapless
    follow me.
They shall be paid with what I win from
    others as from thee.

With the Holy Father's favor we shall live
    after this wise,
Like banished men who have not any grace in
    the King's eyes."

Glad was the Count. For water he asked his
    hands to lave.
And that they brought before him, and
    quickly to him gave.
The Count of Barcelona began to eat his fill
With the men the Cid had given him, and
    God! with what a will!
He who in happy hour was born unto the
    Count sate near:

"Ha! Count, if now thou dinest not with
    excellent good cheer,
And to my satisfaction, here we shall still
    delay,
And we twain in no manner shall go forth
    hence away."
Then said the Count: "Right gladly and
    according to my mind!"
With his two knights at that season in mighty
    haste he dined.
My lord the Cid was well content that all his
    eating eyed,
For the Count don Remónd his hands
    exceeding nimbly plied.

"If thou art pleased, my lord the Cid, in guise

to go are we.
Bid them bring to us our horses; we will
    mount speedily.
Since I was first Count, never have I dined
    with will so glad,
Nor shall it be forgotten what joy therein I
    had."

They gave to them three palfreys. Each had a
    noble selle.
Good robes of fur they gave them, and
    mantles fair as well.
Count don Remónd rode onward with a
    knight on either side.
To the camp's end the Castilian along with
    them
      did ride.

"Ha! Count, forth thou departest to freedom
    fair and frank;
For what thou hast left with me I have thee
    now to thank.
If desire to avenge it is present to thy mind,
Send unto me beforehand when thou comest
    me to find.
Either that thou wilt leave thy goods or part
    of mine wilt seize."

"Ha! my lord Cid, thou art secure, be wholly at
    thine ease.
Enough have I paid to thee till all this year be

gone.

As for coming out to find thee, I will not
think thereon."

LXIII.

The Count of Barcelona spurred forth. Good
speed he made.

Turning his head he looked at them, for he
was much afraid

Lest my lord the Cid repent him; the which
the gallant Cid

Would not have done for all the world. Base
deed he never did.

The Count is gone. He of Bivár has turned
him back again;

He began to be right merry, and he mingled
with his train.

Most great and wondrous was the spoil that
they had won in war,

So rich were his companions that they knew
not what they bore.

CANTAR II

The Marriage of the Cid's Daughters

LXIV.

Here of my lord Cid of Bivár begins anew the
    Song.
Within the pass of Alucát my lord Cid made
    him strong,
He has left Zaragoza and the lands that near
    it lie,
And all the coasts of Montalban and Huésca
    he passed by,
And unto the salt ocean he began the way to
    force.
In the East the sun arises; thither he turned
    his course.
On Jérica and Almenár and Onda he laid hand,
Round about Bórriana he conquered all the
    land.

LXV.

God helped him, the Creator in Heaven that
    doth dwell
Beside these Murviédro hath the Cid ta'en as
    well.
Then that the Lord was on his side, the Cid
    beheld it clear.
In the city of Valencia arose no little fear.

LXVI.

It irked them in Valencia. It gave them no
    delight,

Be it known; that to surround him they
    planned. They marched by night

They pulled up at Murviédro to camp as
    morning broke.

My lord the Cid beheld it and wondering
    much he spoke:

"Father in Heaven, mighty thanks must I now
    proffer Thee.

In their lands we dwell and do them every sort
    of injury;

And we have drunk their liquor, of their bread
    our meal we make.

If they come forth to surround us, justly they
    undertake.

Without a fight this matter will in no way be
    a-paid

Let messengers go seek them who now should
    bear us aid;

Let them go to them in Jérica and Alucát that
    are

And thence to Onda. Likewise let them go to
    Almenár.

Let the men of Bórriana hither at once come
    in.

In this place a pitched battle we shall certainly
    begin.

I trust much will be added to our gain in

this essay."

They all were come together in his host on
    the third day.
And he who in good hour was born 'gan speak
    his meaning clear:

"So may the Creator aid us, my gallants hark
    and hear.
Since we have left fair Christendom—We did
    not as we would;
We could no other—God be praised our
    fortune has been good.
The Valencians besiege us. If here we would
    remain,
They must learn of us a lesson excelling in its
    pain.

LXVII.

"Let the night pass and morning come. Look
    that ye ready be
With arms and horses. We will forth that host
    of theirs to see.
Like men gone out in exile into a strange
    empire,
There shall it be determined who is worthy of
    his hire."

VIII.

Minaya Alvar Fañez, hark what he said
    thereto:

"Ho! Campeador, thy pleasure in all things
    may we do.
Give me of knights an hundred, I ask not one
    other man.
And do thou with the others smite on them in
    the van
While my hundred storm their rearward,
    upon them thou shalt thrust—
Ne'er doubt it. We shall triumph as in God is
    all my trust."
Whatsoever he had spoken filled the Cid with
    right good cheer

And now was come the morning, and they
    donned their battle gear.
What was his task of battle every man of them
    did know.
At the bleak of day against them forth did the
    lord Cid go.
"In God's name and Saint James', my knights,
    strike hard into the war,
And manful. The lord Cid am I, Roy Diaz of
    Bivár!"

You might see a many tent-ropes everywhither
    broken lie,
And pegs wrenched up; the tent-posts on all
    sides leaned awry.
The Moors were very many. To recover they
    were fain,

But now did Alvar Fañez on their rearward
    fall amain.

Though bitterly it grieved them, they had to
    fly and yield.

Who could put trust in horse hoofs, and
    forthwith fled the field.

Two kings of the Moriscos there in the rout
    they slew;

And even to Valencia the chase did they
    pursue.

And mighty is the booty my lord the Cid had
    ta 'en.

They ravaged all the country and then turned
    back again.

They brought to Murviédro the booty of the
    foes.

And great was the rejoicing in the city that
    arose.

Cebólla have they taken and all the lands
    anear.

In Valencia they knew not what to do for very
    fear.

Of my lord Cid the great tidings, be it known,
    on all sides spread.

LXIX.

His renown afar is spreading. Beyond the sea
    it sped.

Glad were the companies the Cid a glad man
    was he

That God had given him succor and gained
  that victory.
And they sent forth their harriers. By night
  they marched away,
They reached unto Culléra, and to Játiva came
  they.
And ever downward even to Dénia town they
  bore.
And all the Moorish country by the sea he
  wasted sore.
Peñacadéll, outgoing and entrance, have they
  ta'en.

LXX.

When the Cid took Peñacadéll, it was great
  grief and pain
To them who in Culléra and in Játiva did
  dwell,
And sorrow without measure in Valencia
  befell.

LXXI.

Three years those towns to conquer in the
  Moorish land he bode,
Winning much; by day he rested, and at night
  was on the road.

LXXII.

On the dwellers in Valencia they wrought
  chastisement sore,
From the town they dared not sally against

him to make war.

He harried all their gardens and a mighty ruin
    made.

And all those years their harvest in utter
    waste he laid.

Loud lamented the Valencians, for sore bested
    they were,

Nor could find in any quarter any sort of
    provender;

Nor could the father aid the son, nor the son
    aid the sire,

Nor comrade comfort comrade. Gentles, 'tis
    hardship dire

To lack for bread, and see our wives and
    children waste away.

They saw their own affliction and no hope of
    help had they.

To the King of Morocco had they sent the
    tidings on.

'Gainst the lord of Montes Claros on a great
    war was he gone.

He counselled not. He came not to aid them in
    the war.

My lord the Cid had heard it. His heart was
    glad therefor;

And forth from Murviédro he marched away
    by night.

He was in the fields of Monreál at the

breaking of the light.

Through Aragon the tidings he published,
and Navarre,

And through the Marches of Castile he spread
the news afar:

Who poverty would put away and riches would
attain,

Let him seek the Cid, whoever of a soldier's
life is fain.

Valencia to beleaguer he desireth to go down,

That he may unto the Christians deliver up
the town

LXXIII.

"Valencia to beleaguer, who fain would march
with me

Let none come hither to me, if his choice be
not free.

Is nought that may compel him along with me
to fare—

Canál de Celfa for three days I will tarry for
him there."

LXXIV.

So my lord Cid hath spoken, the loyal
Campeador.

He turned back to Murviedo that he had ta'en
in war.

Be it known into all quarters went the word
forth. None were fain

To delay who smelt the plunder. Crowds

thronged to him amain,
Good christened folk, and ringing went his
    tidings far and wide;
And more men came unto him than departed
    from his side.
He of Bivár, my lord the Cid, great growth of
    riches had.
When he saw the bands assembled, he began
    to be right glad.
My lord Cid, don Rodrigo, for nothing would
    delay.
He marched against Valencia and smote on it
    straightway.
Well did the Cid surround it; till the leaguer
    closed about.
He thwarted their incomings, he checked
    their goings out.
To seek for alien succor he gave them time of
    grace;
And nine full months together he sat down
    before the place,
And when the tenth was coming, to yield it
    were they fain.

And great was the rejoicing in the city that
    did reign,
When the lord Cid took Valencia and within
    the town had won.
All of his men were cavaliers that erst afoot
    had gone.

Who the worth of gold and silver for your
    pleasure could declare?
They all were rich together as many as were
    there.
For himself the Cid Rodrigo took the fifth
    part of all,
And coined marks thirty thousand unto his
    share did fall.
Who could tell the other treasure? Great joy
    the Cid befell
And his men, when the flag-royal tossed o'er
    the citadel.

LXXV.

The Cid and his companions they rested in
    the place
Unto the King of Seville the tiding came
    apace:
Ta'en is Valencia city; for him 'tis held no
    more.
With thirty thousand armed men he came to
    look them o'er.
Nigh to the plain a battle they pitched both
    stiff and strong.
But the lord Cid long-bearded hath
    overthrown that throng.
And even unto Játiva in a long rout they
    poured.
You might have seen all bedlam on the Jucar
    by the ford,

For there the Moors drank water but sore
    against their will.
With bet thee strokes upon him 'scaped the
    Sovereign of Seville.
And then with all that booty the Cid came
    home again.
Great was Valencia's plunder what time the
    town was ta'en,
But that the spoils of that affray were greater
    yet, know well.
An hundred marks of silver to each common
    soldier fell.
How had shed that noble's fortune now lightly
    may you guess.

LXXVI.

There was among those Christians excelling
    happiness
For my lord Roy Diaz that was born in a
    season of good grace.
And now his beard was growing; longer it
    grew apace.
For this the Cid had spoken, this from his
    mouth said he,
"By my love for King Alphonso the king who
    banished me,"
That the shears should not shear it, nor a
    single hair dispart,
That so the Moors and Christians might
    ponder it at heart.

And resting in Valencia did the lord Cid abide,
With Minaya Alvar Fañez who would not leave
    his side.
They who went forth to exile of riches had
    good store.
To all men in Valencia, the gallant Campeador
Gave houses and possessions whereof they
    were right glad.
All men of the Cid's bounty good testimony
    had.
And of them that had come later well content
    was every one.
My lord Cid saw it plainly that they fain would
    get them gone,
With the goods that they had taken, if
    unhindered they might go.
The lord Cid gave his order (Minaya
    counselled so)
That if any man that with him in richer case
    did stand
Should take his leave in secret and fail to kiss
    his hand,
If they might overtake him and catch him as
    he fled,
They would seize his goods and bring him
    unto the gallows-head.
Lo! was it well looked after. Counsel he took
    again
With Minaya Alvar Fañez "An it be that thou
    art fain,

Gladly would I know, Minaya, what may the
    number be
Of my henchmen, as at present, that have
    gained aught by me.
I shall set it down in writing. Let them well
    the number scan,
Lest one depart in secret and I should miss
    the man.
To me and my companions his goods shall be
    restored,
All they who guard Valencia and keep the
    outer ward.

"The measure is well counselled," said Minaya
    therewithal.

LXXVII.

He bade them meet together at the palace, in
    the hall.
When he found them met together he had
    them numbered o'er.
Bivár's great Cid had with him thousands
    three, and thirty score.
His heart was glad within him, and a smile
    was on his face.
"Thanks be to God, Minaya, and to Mary
    Mother's grace.
Out from Bivár the city we led a lesser power.
Wealth have we, and shall have greater as at
    some later hour.

"Minaya, if it please thee, if it seemeth good
     to thee,
To Castile I fain would send thee, where our
     possessions be,
Unto the King Alphonso that is my lord by
     right.
Out of the mighty plunder we won here in the
     fight
I would give him five score horses, the which
     to him now take;
kiss thou his hand and earnestly plead with
     him for the sake
Of my wife Xiména and the twain, maids of
     my blood that be,
If yet it be his pleasure that they be brought
     to me.

I will send for them. But be it known how this
     my message runs:
The lady of my lord the Cid and her maids, my
     little ones,
Men shall seek for in such fashion that
They shall come to the strange country we
     have conquered by our might."

To him Minaya answered: "Yea and with right
     good heart."
After they thus had spoken they got ready to
     depart.
The Cid to Alvar Fañez an hundred men

decreed

To do his will, and serve him on the journey at
his need.

And he bade give to San Pedro marks of silver
fifty score,

And beside to Abbot Sancho a full five
hundred morn

LXXVIII.

Of these things while they were joyous, came
thither from the East,

A clerk, the Bishop don Jerome, so all men
called that priest.

Excelling was his knowledge, and prudent was
his rede,

'Twas a mighty man of valor afoot or on the
steed.

Of the Cid's deeds the tidings he was seeking
to procure,

And he yearned sore, ever sighing for battle
with the Moor.

If his fill of fight and wounding with his
hands he e'er should get,

Therefore a Christian never need have reason
for regret.

When my lord the Cid had heard it, he was
well pleased thereby:

"Hark, Minaya Alvar Fañez, by him who is on
high,

When the Lord God would aid us, let us give
  Him thanks again.
Round Valencia a bishopric to stablish I am
  fain,
And I will further give it unto this Christian
  leal.
Thou shalt bear with thee good tidings when
  thou goest to Castile."

LXXIX.

Of that saying Alvar Fañez was glad when the
  Cid spake.
Don Jerome his ordination there and then
  they undertake.
In Valencia great riches have they given to his
  hand.
God! how merry was all Christendom that now
  within the land
Of Valencia a bishop of reverend grace had
  they!
Glad therefore was Minaya and took leave and
  went his way.

LXXX.

And now is all Valencia in peaceable estate.
Minaya Alvar Fañez to Castile departed
  straight;
His halts I will pass over, nor renew them to
  the mind.
But he sought out Alphonso where the King

was to find.

The King to Sahagun had gone before some
little space,

But was come back to Carrión; he might find
him in that place.

Minaya Alvar Fañez was glad when this was
known.

With his presents he departed forthwith to
Carrión.

LXXXI.

Now when the mass was over, thence did
Alfonso rise,

And Minaya Alvar Fañez came there in noble
guise.

In the presence of the people he kneeled upon
his knee

He fell at don Alphonso's foot, and bitter tears
shed he.

He kissed his hands; unto the King most
lovely words he spake:

LXXII.

"A boon my lord Alfonso for the Creator's
sake!

My lord Cid of the battles has kissed thy
hands ere now,

Thy hands and thy feet likewise, for his noble
lord art thou,

If thou favorest him, God's favor come upon

thee from above.
Thou didst send him into exile and bearest
    him no love,
Though in strange lands he thriveth. Jérica he
    won in war
And Onda, so they call it; so also Almenár,
And likewise Murviédro (for a greater town
    'tis known),
And he has ta'en Cebólla and further Castejón
And he has stormed Peñacadéll that is a place
    of power.
He is master of Valencia and these places at
    this hour.
With his own hand the great Campeador a
    bishop hath ordained.
He has forced five pitched battles and in each
    three victory gained.
The gift of the Creator was a very mighty
    prey,
Do thou behold the tokens of the truth of
    that I say:
Here be an hundred horses that in strength
    and speed excel;
With bridle and with saddle each one is
    furnished well.
He kissed thy hands and begged thee thine
    acceptance to accord.
He declares himself thy vassal, and owns thee
    for his lord."

The King has lifted his right hand and
    crossed himself thereon:
"With what a wondrous booty the Campeador
    has won
I am well pleased in spirit. Saint Isidore to
    speed!
I am glad the Campeador does now so many a
    fair deed.
I accept the gift of horses that the Cid to me
    has sent"
Though the King thereby was gladdened, was
    Ordoñez not content;

"Meseems that in the Moorish land is no man
    any more,
Since so his will upon them works the Cid
    Campeador."

To the Count the King gave answer: "So speak
    not of him now!
In faith he doth me service of a better sort
    than thou."

And then outspoke Minaya, like a nobleman
    spoke he:
"The Cid, if it shall please thee, desires a boon
    of thee,
For his wife Dame Xiména and his daughters
    two beside,
That they may leave the convent where he left
    them to abide,

And may hasten to Valencia to the noble
    Campeador."
Then said the King in answer: "My heart is
    glad therefor.
That they be given escort I will issue the
    command,
So that they may be protected as they travel
    through my land
From insult and dishonor and whatever harm
    may be.
And when these ladies shall have reached my
    kingdom's boundary,
Have a care how thou shalt serve them, thou
    and the Campeador.
Now hark to me, my vassals, and my courtiers
    furthermore:
I like not that to Roy Diaz any losses shall
    befall,
And therefore to his vassals, the Cid their lord
    that call,
I restore that which I seized on, their
    possession and their fee.
Let them keep their lands, no matter where
    the Campeador may be
From harm and hurt the safety of their
    persons I accord.
This I do that they may lightly render service
    to their lord."

Minaya Alvar Fañez kissed the King's hand

straightway.

And the King smiled upon him and a fair
    word did he say:

''Who'er to serve the Campeador desireth now
    to ride,

As for me, he has permission, and God's grace
    with him abide.

More than by further hatred by this measure
    shall we gain.''

Counsel straightway together held the Heirs
    of Carrión twain.

"The fame of the Cid Campeador grows great
    on every side,

An we might wed his daughters, would our
    needs be satisfied.

Scarce we dare frame this project e'en to
    ourselves alone;

The Cid is of Bivár, and we are Counts of
    Carrión."

They hatched that plot between them, to none
    they told the thing.

Minaya Alvar Fañez took leave of the good
    King:

"Ha! goest thou, Minaya? The Creator give
    thee grace.

Take an herald. As I deem it he may help thee
    in this case.

If thou take the ladies, serve them even as

they desire.

Even unto Medína grant them all that they
require.

The Campeador shall take them in his charge
thenceforward on."

After leave ta'en Minaya from the court he
got him gone.

LXXXIII.

And so the Heirs of Carrión did each with
each consent.

With Minaya Alvar Fañez in company they
went:

"In all things thou excellest; likewise in this
excel:

Greet now my lord Cid of Bivár for us
exceeding well,

To the utmost of our effort his partisans are
we.

The Cid, an he will love us, shall get no
injury."

Said Minaya: "In that proffer naught
displeasing I discern."

Gone is Minaya. Home again did the two
counts return.

He hastens to San Pedro where the three
ladies are.

Very great was the rejoicing when they saw
him from afar.

To offer prayer Minaya to San Pedro did
    descend.
He turned back unto the ladies when the
    prayer was at an end.
"I greet thee, Dame Xiména. God thee prosper
    and maintain,
And so likewise thy daughters, the noble
    children twain.
In the city where he dwelleth the lord Cid
    greets thee fair.
Good health has he and riches that are
    beyond compare.
The King for a gift to him your freedom gave
    to me,
To take you to Valencia our land of lawful fee.
If the Cid might behold you well and
    unharmed again,
He would be all rejoicing, but scant would be
    his pain."
"May the Creator so decide," the Dame
    Xiména said.
Minaya Alvar Fañez sent three horsemen on
    ahead,
To the Cid within Valencia the men did he
    commend:
"Announce unto the Campeador, whom the
    Lord God defend,
That the King his wife and daughters has
    released unto my hands,
And has ordered escort for us as we travel

through his lands.
Fifteen days from this time forwar, if God
keep us in his care,
With his wife and with his daughters I will
come unto him there,
With the noble ladies also their servitors that
be."
The riders are gone forward, to the matter
they will see.

Minaya Alvar Fañez in San Pedro did abide.
There might you see the household swarming
in from every side;
Unto my lord Cid of Bivár in Valencia would
they go.
They besought Alvar Fañez that he would
them favor so.
To them replied Minaya. "That will I gladly
do."
And five and sixty horsemen have swelled his
retinue,
And he had brought an hundred thither in his
command.
To accompany the ladies, they arrayed a noble
band.

Minaya marks five hundred to the Abbot then
gave o'er.
I will tell how he expended other five and
twenty score.

Xiména the good lady and likewise her
    daughters twain,
And they that served before her, the women
    of her train,
To deck out all those ladies good Minaya did
    prepare
With the best array in Burgos, that he might
    discover there,
And the mules and palfreys likewise that they
    might be fair to see.
When he had decked the ladies in this manner
    beautifully,
Got ready good Minaya to ride upon his way.
Lo now! Raquél and Vidas. Down at his feet
    fell they:
"A boon! true knight, Minaya! If the Cid stand
    not our aid,
He has ruined us. If only the amount to us
    were paid
We would forego the usury!" "So will I tell the
    Cid,
If God bring me there. High favor shall there
    be for what ye did."
Answered Raquél and Vidas: "The Creator
    send it so.
If not, we will leave Burgos in search of him to
    go."

Minaya Alvar Fañez to San Pedro got him
    gone.

Many people came around him as he started
    to ride on.
At parting from the Abbot great grief of
    heart was there:
"Minaya Alvar Fañez, God keep thee in his
    care.
The hands of the good Campeador, I prithee
    kiss for me
That he may keep the convent still in his
    memory,
And always may endeavor to make it prosper
    more,
So shall increase the honor of the Cid
    Campeador."
"Right gladly will I do it," Minaya straight
    replied.
Their leave then have they taken and fettled
    them to ride,
And with them went the herald on their need
    that was to wait.
Through the King's realm an escort they gave
    them very great.
From San Pedro to Medína in five days time
    they passed.
Lo, the dames and Alvar Fañez to Medína
    came at last!

I will tell you of the horsemen that brought
    those tidings through.
When my lord the good Cid of Bivár thereof

the import knew,

He was glad at heart and merry. His voice he
    lifted straight:

"Who sends a noble messenger, should like
    return await.

Munio Gustióz, Per Vermudóz, the first of all
    are you,

And Martin Antolínez from Burgos, tried and
    true,

And Jerome the bishop also, a worthy clerk is
    he,

With a hundred ride you ready to fight if need
    shall be.

Through Saint Mary's to Molína further
    onward shall ye wend;

Avelgalvon there holds sway my vassal and my
    friend.

With another hundred horsemen he will
    watch you on your way.

Ride forth unto Medína with all the speed ye
    may,

With Minaya Alvar Fañez my wife and
    daughters there

Haply ye shall discover as the messengers
    declare.

Bring them hither to me nobly. In Valencia I
    will bide,

That cost me dear. Unguarded 'twere madness
    undenied

To leave it. 'Tis my portion. There will I stay

therefore."
They fettled them for riding, when all his
    words were o'er;

With utmost speed they hastened, their
    march they would not stay.
They have passed by Saint Mary's. At
    Fronchále rested they.
Next day into Molína, their halting-place, they
    spurred.
When those tidings the Morisco Avengalvón
    had heard,
To welcome them with joyance unto them did
    he descend:
"Are you then come the vassals of my heart's
    dearest friend?
Be it known it grieves me little. Therein my
    joy is great."

And Muño Gustióz answered, for no man
    would he wait:
"My lord Cid sends thee greeting, as also his
    command
That with an hundred horsemen thou shalt
    serve him out of hand.
In the city of Medína lie his wife and
    danghters twain.
Thou wilt go for them straightway and bring
    them here again,
Even unto Valencia thou shalt not from them

part."

Avengalvón gave answer: "I will do it with glad
    heart."

That night he chose them escort, a mighty
    band were they.

In the morning they got ready anew to take
    the way.

They asked for but an hundred; ten score had
    he forby.

They passed across the mountains that were
    so steep and high,

And through the thicket of Toránz, so strong
    they had no dread.

And along through Arbujuélo adown the vale
    they sped.

Now round about Medína they watched on
    every side,

Minaya Alvar Fañez that armed train descried.

He was afraid and sent two knights the
    meaning to make plain.

They delayed not, to discover his desire their
    hearts were fain.

One stayed, to Alvar Fañez the other came
    once more:

"A company to seek us comes from the
    Campeador.

Per Vermudóz, lo, foremost among those
    ranks is he,

And likewise Muño Gustióz that frankly

loveth thee,
And Martin Antolínez that was born in
    Burgos town,
And don Jerome the Bishop of honorable
    renown.
Avellgalvon the Castellan bringeth his host
    with these,
In eagerness the honor of my lord Cid to
    increase.
They march along together. They will be here
    anon."
Said Minaya: "Forth now let us ride." And
    swiftly was it done,
They would not stay. An hundred most
    splendidly arrayed
Sallied forth on noble horses with trappings
    of brocade.
Bells hung upon the martingales, the knights
    their bucklers bore
At the neck, and carried lances whence flew
    the flags of war
That Alvar Fañez' wisdom to all they might
    reveal,
And in what guise with those ladies he had
    issued from Castile.
All they that reconnoitering before the army
    ran
Now lifted up their weapons, and to make
    good cheer began.
Great mirth was there when all the rest to the

Jalón drew nigh.

When they came unto Minaya they did him
 homage high.

And when Avengalvón was come, and might
 Minaya see,

Then forward to embrace him with smiling
 lips came he.

On the shoulder he saluted him, for such was
 still his way:

"O Minaya Alvar Fañez! For thee what glorious
 day!

Thou bringest here these ladies, whence we
 shall have great good,

The fighting Cid his consort, and the
 daughters of his blood.

We all shall do thee honor for his fortune
 groweth great.

Though we wished him ill, we cannot
 diminish his estate;

He will have alway our succor either in peace
 or war.

The man who will not know the truth, he is a
 dolt therefor."

LXXXIV.

Minaya Alvar Fañez, on his lips a smile broke
 out:

"Ha now! Ha now! Avengalvón. Thou art his
 friend no doubt.

If God shall bring me to the Cid and him alive

I see,
The things that thou has done for us shall
    greatly profit thee.
Let us to our lodging, supper they have made
    ready there."
Avengalvón gave answer: "Tis a courtesy most
    fair;
Double will I repay it ere the third morning
    fall."
To the town they came. Minaya provided for
    them all.
The escort that came with them, they were
    gladdened when they saw.
Minaya the King's herald commanded to
    withdraw.
The lord Cid in Valencia was greatly honored
    then,
When they gave such entertainment in
    Medína to his men.
The King paid for all. Minaya therefor had
    naught to pay.

At length the night was over, and came the
    break of day.
And mass they heard, and after away they
    rode at last.
They hastened from Medína, o'er the Jalón
    they passed.
And down the Arbujuélo, spurring apace they
    ride.

In haste the meadows of Toránz they cross
    from side to side,
They came unto Molína where Avengalvón
    was lord.
Bishop Jerome, a Christian worthy of his deed
    and word,
Escorted the three ladies whether by day or
    night,
And he led a good charger with his armor on
    his right.
And he and Alvar Fañez rode aye together
    thus.
They have entered in Molína the rich and
    glorious,
And loyally Avengalvón the Moor has served
    them there.
Unto the height of their desire, nothing they
    lacked whatever:
He even bade men strike for them the
    horseshoe from the steed.
Minaya and the ladies, God! he honored them
    indeed
They got them upon horseback when the next
    morning fell.
Unto Valencia loyally he served them all and
    well.

The Moor spent of his own estate, for naught
    from them took he.
With such honorable matters and mirth and

revelry
They came nigh unto Valencia, that three
    leagues off doth stand.
To my lord Cid who in good hour had girded
    on the brand,
In the city of Valencia the news thereof they
    bore.

LXXXV.

Nothing had ever gladdened him so much as
    this or more,
For now there came good news of them for
    whom great love he had.
Straightway two hundred horsemen to go
    forth to them he bade,
To the good dames and Minaya fair reception
    to afford.
But he tarried in Valencia to watch it and to
    ward,
For he knew that Alvar Fañez with all due
    care would come.

LXXXVI.

And lo! now the two hundred welcomed
    Minaya home.
And the ladies and the daughters and all
    within the band.
The Cid to them within his train had issued
    his command
To ward full well the citadel, and the towers

that were so high,
And the gates that none might enter and
    none depart thereby.
And he bade bring Baviéca that a little time
    before
From the King of Seville he had taken, when
    he routed him in war.
The Cid that in good season girt the brand
    on, of that steed
Knew not if he were swift to run or to stop
    short at need.
At the gateway of Valencia where none might
    work him woe,
Unto his wife and daughters he desired his
    gear to show.

When the ladies with great honor the host
    had welcomed home,
Then first into the city came the Bishop don
    Jerome.
He left his horse; to chapel straightway the
    Bishop went.
With all men that he could gather who were
    of like intent
And surplice-clad, with crosses of silver, once
    again
They greeted good Minaya and the ladies of
    the train.
He who was born in happy time tarried but
    little there.

He has put on his surcoat. His beard was long
　　and fair.
On Baviéca saddle and caparisons they threw.
The Cid took wooden weapons; forth on the
　　steed he flew.
Leaped the steed Baviéca. With a great rush
　　did he run.
'Twas rare to see. And when he ceased they
　　marvelled all and one.
From that day Baviéca in all Spain had
　　renown.
When that career was ended, from the steed
　　the Cid got down,
And hastened forth his lady and daughters
　　twain to greet.
When Dame Xiména saw him she cast her at
　　his feet:
"Brand thou girdest in good season. Thy
　　favour, Campeador!
Thou hast brought me forth from insults that
　　were exceeding sore.
Look on me, lord! Look also on my daughters
　　as on me.
By God's help and thine they are noble, and
　　gently reared they be.

And the Cid straightway embraced them,
　　mother and daughters twain.
Such joy they had that from their eyes the
　　tears began to rain.

His men rejoiced. The quintains, they pierced
them with the spear.
He who girt sword in a good time, hark what
he said and hear.

"Oh thou my Dame Xiména, beloved and
honored wife,
And ye two both my daughters that are my
heart and life,
To the city of Valencia now do yet enter in,
The fair estate that for you it was my lot to
win."

His hands they have kissed straightway, the
daughters and their dame.
So with exceeding honor to Valencia they
came.

LXXXVII.

With them the lord Cid hastened to the
citadel apace,
He has ta'en the ladies straightway up to the
highest place.
And forth in all directions they turn their
lovely eyes,
And they behold Valencia and how the city
lies,
And in another quarter they might perceive
the sea.
They look on fertile meadows close sown and
great that be,

And on all things whatever that were of fair
    estate
God they praised with hands uplifted for that
    good prize and great.

My lord Cid and his followers thereof were
    glad and fain.
And now was winter over, for March would
    come again.
And of the countries oversea 'tis my desire to
    tell,
Even of the King Yússuf in Morocco that did
    dwell.

LXXVIII.

The King's heart of Morocco 'gainst the Cid
    was full of rage.
"By force the man hath entered into my
    heritage,
And giveth thanks to no one save Jesus Christ
    therefor."

And the King of Morocco gathered his hosts
    of war.
With fifty times a thousand under arms, good
    men and stark,
They put to sea. In galleons that army did
    embark
To seek the Cid Rodrigo in Valencia they
    went,
The ships came in; and straightway issued

forth that armament.

LXXXIX.

To Valencia that the Cid had ta'en, 'twas
thither they did fare.

The unbelievers halted and pitched pavilions
there.

With tidings of the chances to my lord the Cid
they came.

XC.

"Now thanks to the Creator and the Holy
Father's name.

All the goods in my possession, I have them
here with me.

Hardly I took Valencia, but I hold it for my
fee;

This side death, I cannot yield it. Glory to God
again

And to Holy Mary Mother that my wife and
daughters twain

Are here with me. From oversea cometh now
my delight.

Never will I forego it, I will take the arms of
fight.

My lady and my daughters shall see me lift
the brand,

They shall see how men build houses here in a
foreign land,

And how a livelihood is won their eyes shall
see it well."

He took his wife and daughters up to the
    citadel.
They raised their eyes and men they saw
    pitching tents everywhere.
"Cid, what is this? So may the Lord still keep
    thee in His care."
"Ha, wife, much honored! Therefor prithee be
    not troubled thus.
'Tis wealth most great and wondrous that
    they gather here for us.
Scarce art thou come, when presents they
    would give thee in that hour.
Thy daughters wait for marriage 'tis these
    that bring the dower."
"Unto thee, Cid, and unto God do I give
    thanks again"
"My lady in the palace in the citadel remain.
When thou seest me in battle, fear not at all
    for me.
By Saint Mary Mother's mercy, by God His
    charity,
That thou art here before me, my heart grows
    great within.
With God His help, this battle I certainly shall
    win."

XCI.
Now pitched are the pavilions. Apace the
    morning comes.
And furiously the heathen beat loud upon the

drums.

"Tis a great day," with a glad heart so now the
    lord Cid spake.

But his lady was sore frighted, her heart was
    like to break;

The ladies and his daughters were likewise all
    forlorn.

Never had they heard such a din since the day
    when they were born.

Therewith the great Cid Campeador with his
    hand he plucked his beard.

"This shall all be to your vantage. Therefore
    be not afeard.

Ere fifteen days are over, if so God's will it be,

We shall take those drums and show them
    you.

What they are then shall you see.

And then unto the Bishop don Jerome they
    shall be given;

They will hang them in Saint Mary's, Mother
    of the Lord in Heaven."

It was a vow most solemn that my lord the Cid
    had made.

Now merry were the ladies and not so much
    afraid.

Those Moors out of Morocco in mighty haste
    they sped,

And on into the gardens they entered

without dread.

XCII.

That thing beheld the outpost. He let the
    tocsin sound.
Of the Cid Roy Diaz ready were the companies
    around.
They sallied from the city with their arms
    appointed well.
When they came on the Moriscos upon them
    swift they fell.
They drove them from the gardens in
    exceeding sorry plight;
Of the Moors a full five hundred they
    slaughtered in that fight.

XCIII.

Even to the pavilions the pursuers would not
    slack;
They had done much and nobly when they
    thought of turning back.
There Alvar Salvadórez a prisoner did remain.
Then those that ate his bread returned to the
    lord Cid again.
With his own eyes he beheld it, to his face
    they spake thereon;
My lord the Cid was gladdened of the deeds
    that they had done.
"My knights we cannot other. Then harken
    unto me:
'Tis a noble day, yet nobler will tomorrow's

battle be.
Arm you ere dawn. The Bishop don Jerome
   our souls will shrive,
Saying mass for us ere at them we are ready to
   let drive.
It shall be in no other fashion, we will go
   smite the foe,
In God's name and his Apostle's the good
   Saint James also.
For better fight than let them in the land
   devour our bread."
"With a good will and gladly," in reply to him
   they said.

And then outspake Minaya, for nothing
   tarried he:
"Since thou wishest this, give orders of
   another sort to me.
For the sore need of battle grant me six score
   horse and ten;
From the far flank, when thou charges will I
   fall on them then.
On one side or the other the Lord will stand
   our stead."
"With right good will," unto him answered
   the Cid and said.

XCIV.
And now broke forth the morning, and now
   drew back the night.
Those bands of Christ delayed not to get

ready for the fight.

At the middle cocks ere morning, mass for
them Jerome did chant,

And mass said, absolution in full to them did
grant:

"Who face to face shall perish this day the
fight within,

May Christ receive his spirit, on my soul I take
his sin.

Cid, don Rodrigo, in good hour thou girdedst
brand; to thee

I sang the mass this morning. Grant then my
boon to me:

Give me to strike the foremost the first stroke
of the war."

"The thing to thee is granted," answered the
Campeador.

XCV.

Out through the Quarter Towers full armed
away they went.

The lord Cid and his henchmen did counsel
and consent.

Levies they left behind them, the gates to
watch and keep.

On the steed Baviéca sprang the lord Cid with
a leap.

Fair trappings and caparisons girded that
steed about.

With the standard from Valencia forthwith

they sallied out.
Were with the Cid four thousand less but a
 score and ten,
They came gladly to a battle against fifty
 thousand men.
Alvar Alvarez and Minaya on the other side
 did smite.
It seemed good to the Creator, and they threw
 them into flight.
With the lance the Cid did battle, hand he set
 to sword as well.
So many Moors he slaughtered that their
 numbers none might tell.
Down from his elbow streaming the blood of
 battle came.
Even against King Yússuf three buffets did he
 aim.
He 'scaped from underneath the sword for his
 steed could run apace,
And bore him to Culléra, an exceeding mighty
 place.
Even so far he of Bivár pursued them as they
 fled,
With a host of gallant vassals in his company
 that sped.
He who in happy hour was born from that
 pursuit turned back;
He was gladdened of the booty they had taken
 in the attack.
Good to him seemed Baviéca from head to tail

that day.
In his hands remained the booty of that battle
    for a prey.
Of the twoscore and ten thousand, when they
    were counted o'er,
There 'scaped out of that battle but an
    hundred men and four.
My lord the Cid his henchmen have sacked the
    field around;
Of the gold and of the silver three thousand
    marks they found,
And of the other booty was no measure to be
    had.
My lord Cid and his vassals were all exceeding
    glad,
For in winning of the battle God's grace to
    them was shown,
When the king of Morocco in this guise was
    overthrown.
The Cid left Alvar Fañez to count the spoil
    and slain.
With fivescore horse he entered Valencia once
    again.
Helmless he rode. Upon his brow the coif was
    disarrayed.
Through the town on Baviéca he galloped,
    hand on blade.
And the ladies gave him welcome, on his
    coming that did wait.
My lord Cid stopped before them, reining in

the charger great:

"Ladies, I bow before you. Groweth apace my
    fame.

While you have held Valencia in the field I
    overcame.

This was our God's desire and all his Saints
    likewise,

Since at your coming hither He gave us such a
    prize.

Look on the bloody sword-blade and the steed
    with sweat a-foam.

With such are the Moriscos in the battle
    overcome.

Pray now to God that I may yet live some few
    years from this;

You shall enter to great honor and men your
    hands shall kiss."

So he spake as he dismounted. When on the
    ground stood he

When the dames and his daughters and his
    wife of high degree

Saw him get off, they kneeled them down
    before the Campeador:

"Thy will be done, and mayst thou live
    through many a long year more."

The Cid unto the palace returning then they
    brought;

They rested them on benches most exquisitely

wrought:

"Ha! Dame Xiména, wife of mine, didst thou
    beg this of me?

These dames thou hast brought hither so well
    that wait on thee,

In marriage to my vassals I am fain to give
    them o'er,

And unto every lady for her dower marks ten
    score.

Men shall know of their good service, in the
    kingdom of Castile.

With my maids' affairs hereafter at our
    leisure we shall deal."

All there rose up together, and kissed his
    fingers straight,

The rejoicing in the palace it was exceeding
    great.

As my lord Cid commanded so they brought
    the thing about.

Minaya Alvar Fañez tarried on the field
    without,

With his men to write and reckon. Arms, tents
    and rich array

In great store they discovered. It was a sovran
    prey.

The richest of the treasure I am fain now to
    recite:

The tale of all the horses they could not take
    aright;

They wandered all caparisoned. Was none to
    take a steed.
The Moors out of their provinces had
    gathered wealth indeed.
Though this were so, were given to the gallant
    Campeador
Of the best of all the horses for his share fifty
    score.
When the Cid had so many the rest content
    might bide.
What store of rich pavilions and carven poles
    beside
To the lord Cid and his vassals by the chance
    of war did fall,
And the King's tent of Morocco was the
    richest of them all,
All gold wrought are the tent-poles that
    pavilion that sustain.
My lord Cid the great Campeador did at that
    time ordain
That it stand pitched; to move it let not a
    Christian dare.
"Since hither from Morocco is come a tent so
    fair,
To Alfonso the Castilian I am fain to send it
    now;
That the Cid hath captured somewhat then
    lightly will be trow."

Laden with mighty riches to Valencia came

they home.

That very noble cleric, the Bishop don Jerome,

When a surfeit of the fighting he had had of
his hands twain,

Was at a loss to number the Moors that he had
slain.

What fell to him of booty was sovran great of
worth.

My lord Cid don Rodrigo (in a good time was
his birth,)

Of all his fifth share of the spoil has sent him
the tenth part.

XCVI.

The Christians in Valencia were all right glad
of heart,

For now excelling riches, horses and arms
they had.

Xiména and her daughters all three were
passing glad,

And the other dames; as wedded upon
themselves looked they.

And my lord Cid the noble in no wise would
delay.

"Where art thou brave Minaya? Come hither
to me now.

For thy great share of booty, no gratitude hast
thou?

Of this my fifth of all the prey, I tell thee clear
and plain,

Take unto thy good pleasure, but let the rest
    remain.
And tomorrow in the morning thou shalt
    certainly ride out
With the horses of my portion that I captured
    in the rout,
With the saddles and the bridles and the
    swords that them behove,
For the sake of my lady and for my daughters
    love.
Since Alfonso sent the ladies whither they
    were content,
These same two hundred horses to him thou
    shalt present,
That of him who rules Valencia the King no ill
    may say."

He bade go with Minaya Per Vermudóz
    straightway.
The next day in the morning they departed
    with all speed,
And a full two hundred henchmen along with
    them they lead,
With greetings from the Cid who fain would
    kiss his hands aright.
Even out of the battle where my lord Cid won
    the fight,
For a gift he sent Alfonso of horses good ten
    score:
"While I have breath within me, I will serve

him evermore."

XCVII.

They have issued from Valencia. And they
    fettle them to fare.

They must watch well so mighty a booty do
    they bear.

And night and day they hastened for they
    gave themselves no rest.

The mountains that divide the lauds they
    have passed o'er the crest.

And the folk they fell to asking where
    Alfonso.

XCVIII.

O'er the mountains, o'er the rivers, o'er the
    hills they took the road.

And at length before Valladolíd where the
    King lay they were.

Minaya and Per Vermudóz sent tidings to him
    there,

That reception to their followers he might bid
    his men extend.

"My lord Cid of Valencia presents with us doth
    send."

XCIX.

Glad was the King. Man gladder you never yet
    did see.

He commanded all his nobles to ride forth
    hastily.

And forth among the first of them did King
     Alfonso go,
Of him who in good hour was born the
     tidings for to know.
Know you the Heirs of Carrión happed in that
     place to be,
Also Count don García the Cid's worst enemy.
Of the tidings some were merry, and some
     were all folorn.
They caught sight of his henchmen who in
     happy hour was born.
They feared it was an army for no herald came
     before.
Straightway the King Alfonso crossed himself
     o'er and o'er.
Minaya and Per Vermudóz came forward with
     all speed,
They leaped from the saddle, they dismounted
     from the steed.
Before the King Alfonso upon their knees
     they fell.
They kissed the ground beneath him, they
     kissed his feet as well:
"Now a boon, King Alfonso. Thou art great
     and glorious.
For my lord Cid the Campeador do we
     embrace thee thus.
He holds himself thy vassal; he owns thee for
     his lord.
He prizes high the honor thou didst to him

accord.

O King, but a few days agone in the fight he
    overcame

The King out of Morocco, Yússuf (that is his
    name),

With a host of fifty thousand from the field
    he drove away.

The booty that he captured was a great and
    sovran prey.

Great wealth unto his followers because of
    this did fall.

He sends thee twoscore horses and doth kiss
    thy hands withal.

Said King Alfonso:

"Gladly to accept them am I fain.

To the Cid who sent me such a gift I send my
    thanks again.

When I do unto his liking, may he live to see
    the day."

Thereat were many of good cheer and kissed
    his hands straightway.

Grieved was Count don García. Wroth was his
    heart within.

Apart he wells a little with ten men of his kin:

"A marvel is this matter of the Cid, so grows
    his fame.

Now by the honor that he hath we shall be put
    to shame.

Kings he o'erthroweth lightly, and lightly

bringeth steeds
As though he dead had found them; we are
    minished by his deeds."

C.
Hear now of King Alfonso what he said upon
    this score:
"Thanks be to the Creator and the lord Saint
    Isidore
For the two hundred horses that the Cid to
    me hath sent.
Yet shall he serve me better in this my
    government.
To Minaya Alvar Fañez and Per Vermudóz I
    say
That you forthwith clothe your bodies in
    honorable array,
And as you shall require it of me take battle-
    gear
Such as before Roy Diaz in good manner shall
    appear.
Take then the gift I give you even these
    horses three.
As it seems to my avisement, as my heart
    telleth me,
Out of all these adventures some good will
    come to light."

CI.
They kissed his hands and entered to take
    their rest that night.

In all things that they needed he bade men
    serve them well.

Of the two Heirs of Carrión now am I fain to
    tell,
How secretly they counselled what thing
    should be their cast:
"Of my lord Cid the high affairs go forward
    wondrous fast.
Let us demand his daughters that with them
    we may wed.
Our fortune and our honor thereby may be
    well sped."
Unto the King Alfonso with their secret forth
    went they.

CII.

"As from our King and master a boon of thee
    we pray
By favor of thy counsel we desire to obtain
That thou ask for us in marriage of the Cid
    his daughters twain.
With honor and with profit shall the match
    for then, be fraught."

Thereon for a full hour's space pondered the
    King and thought
"I cast out the good Campeador, and wrong I
    do him still
For his good to me. I know not if the match be
    to his will,

But we in hand will take it, since so your
    pleasures tend."

Alvar Fañez and Per Vermudóz, for them the
    King let send.
He took them to a hall apart: "Now harken to
    me both
Minaya and Per Vermudóz. The Cid my service
    doth;
The Campeador, his pardon well hath he
    earned of me.
And shall have it. I will meet him, if so his will
    shall be.
In parley other tidings of my court I will make
    known;
Dídago and Ferrándo, the Heirs of Carrión,
Are fain to wed his daughters. Bear ye the
    message well,
And I pray you that these tidings to the
    Campeador ye tell.
It will be unto his honor, great will his fame
    have grown,
When he becomes the father of the Heirs of
    Carrión."

Minaya spake: (Per Vermudóz was glad of that
    he spake)
"To ask him thy desire we will even undertake.
And the Cid shall do thereafter as his pleasure
    shall decide."

"Say to the Cid Roy Diaz that was born in a
    glad tide,
That I will parley with him in the best place
    he may,
And there shall be the boundary wherever he
    shall say.
To my lord Cid in all things will I show my
    favor plain."

Unto the King they gave farewell, and got
    them gone again,
And onward to Valencia they hastened with
    their force.

When the good Campeador had heard, swiftly
    he got to horse,
And came to meet them smiling, and strong,
    embraced the two.
"Minaya and Per Vermudóz, ye are come back
    anew!
There are not many countries where two such
    gallants dwell.
From my lord King Alfonso what tidings are
    to tell?
Is he content? Did he vouchsafe to take the
    gift from me?"

Said Minaya, "In his soul and heart right well
    content is he,
And his good will he sendeth unto thee
    furthermore."

Said the Cid: "To the Creator now mighty
    thanks therefor."

The Leonese Alfonso his pleasure they made
    known
That the Cid should give his daughters to the
    Heirs of Carrión.
He deemed it would make him glorious and
    cause his fame to grow.
And in all truth and honor would advise him
    even so.

When my lord the Cid had heard it, the noble
    Campeador,
Then a long time much pondering he turned
    the tidings o'er,
"For this to Christ my master do I give thanks
    again.
I was sent forth to exile and my honor
    suffered stain.
That which is mine I conquered by mine
    endeavor high.
Unto God for the King's favor a thankful man
    am I,
And that for them of Carrión they ask my
    daughters two.
Minaya and Per Vermudóz, thereof what
    thinketh you?"

"Whate'er shall be your pleasure, that is it we
    shall say."

Said the Cid: "The Heirs of Carrión, of a great
    line are they,
And they are proud exceeding, and their favor
    fair at court.
Yet ill doth such a marriage with my desire
    coport.
But since it is his pleasure that is of more
    worth than we,
Let us talk thereof a little, but secret let us
    be.
May the Lord God in Heaven accord us as is
    best."

"Besides all this Alfonso this word to thee
    addressed:
He would come to parley with thee in what
    place thou art fain.
He desireth well to see thee and honor thee
    again.
Then what to do is fittest ye might be well
    agreed."

Said the Cid: "Now by this saying I am well
    pleased indeed."

"Where thou wilt hold this parley" said
    Minaya, "ponder well.
"In that the king desired it, no wondrous
    thing befell,"
That wherever we might find him we might
    seek him in his way,

As to our King and Master, our high devoir to
    pay.
Haply we may desire what good to him shall
    seem.
Nigh to the river Tagus that is a noble stream,
If so my lord desire it, we will hold the parley
    there."

He wrote the letters straightway and sealed
    them well and fair.
And then unto two horsemen he gave the
    letters o 'er.
Whatso the King desireth, that will the
    Campeador.

CIII.
Unto the King much honored, the letters they
    present.
When he had looked upon them, then was his
    heart content.
"To the Cid who in good time girt brand my
    greeting do I send,
And let us hold the parley when three weeks
    are at an end.
If I yet live, then doubtless I shall wait him in
    that place."
They tarried not, but hastened home to the
    Cid apace.

On both sides for the parley they got ready
    point device.

In Castile was ne'er such foison of mules
    without a price,
Nor so many fair-paced palfreys, nor strong
    steeds swift to guide,
Nor so many noble pennons on the stout
    lances tied,
And shields whereof the bosses did with gold
    and silver shine,
Robes, furs and Alexandrian cloth of satin
    woven fine.
And the King gave his order, to send much
    victual there,
To the waters of the Tagus where the parley
    they prepare.
The King leads many a good troop, and
    Carrión's Heirs are gay.
And here they run in debt apace, and there
    again they pay,
For they thought to have great profit and
    increase manifold,
And whatso they should desire, goods of silver
    and of gold.
And now hath King Alfonso got swiftly to his
    horse,
With counts and little nobles and vassals in
    great force.
As for the Heirs of Carrión great companies
    they bring.
From León and from Galicia came much
    people with the King;

Know well, the levies of Castile, they are a
    countless train.
And straight unto the parley they rode with
    slackened rein.

CIV.

In the city of Valencia, my lord Cid Campeador
Did not tarry, but the parley, he prepared
    himself therefor.
There were stout mules a-many and palfreys
    swift to course,
Great store of goodly armour, and many a
    fleet war-horse,
Many fair cloaks and mantles, and many skins
    withal;
In raiment of all colors are clad both great
    and small.
Minaya Alvar Fañez and Per Vermudóz that
    wight,
Martin Muñoz in Montemayór that held the
    rule of right,
And Martin Antolínez that in Burgos had his
    home,
And that most worthy cleric, the Bishop don
    Jerome,
And with Alvar Salvadórez Alvar Alvarez
    beside,
And likewise Muño Gustióz a gallant knight
    and tried,
Also Galínd Garcíaz, that in Aragon abode,

These to ride with the good Campeador got
  ready for the road.
And the people in the palace prepared them
  all and one.

Unto Alvar Salvadórez and the man of Aragon,
Galínd Garcíaz, his command has given the
  Campeador
That heart and soul Valencia they shall guard
  it and watch o'er.
And, moreover, all the others on their behests
  shall wait.
And my lord Cid has ordered that they bar the
  castle gate
And nowise throw it open either by night or
  day.
His wife and his two daughters within the
  hold are they,
Whom he loves best, and the ladies that do
  their pleasure still.
And he has so disposed it, even as a good lord
  will,
That not a soul among them shall venture
  from the tower,
Till to them he returneth, who was born in
  happy hour.

They issued from Valencia, forward they
  spurred along.
On their right were many horses, that were

both swift and strong.
The Cid had ta 'en them. No man would have
    given him a steed.
And he rideth to the parley, the which he had
    decreed
With the King. In passage of a day, he came
    the King before.
When anear they saw him coming, the gallant
    Campeador,
With great worship to receive him, forth unto
    him they ride.
When he had looked upon them, who was
    born in a glad tide,
He halted his companions save his knights of
    dearest worth.
With fifteen of his henchmen he leaped down
    unto the earth,
As he who in good hour was born had willed
    that it should be.
Forthwith to earth he bends him on the hand
    and on the knee.
And the grass of the meadow with his very
    teeth he rent,
And wept exceeding sorely so great was his
    content.
How well unto Alfonso to do homage doth he
    know
And there before his sovereign's foot he cast
    him even so.
As for the King Alfonso, at heart it irked

him sore:

"Rise up! Rise up upon thy feet, O thou Cid
 Campeador,
And kiss my hand, nor prithee in this guise
 my feet embrace,
And if thou wilt not do it, thou shalt not have
 my grace."
But natheless the good Campeador yet knelt
 on bended knee:
"As of my rightful master, I ask a boon of thee,
And namely that thy favor on me thou wilt
 bestow,
So that all men about us the thing may hear
 and know."

Said the King: "Now that right gladly and of
 good heart will I do;
And here I give thee pardon, and my favor I
 renew.
And thee unto my kingdom right welcome I
 will make."

My lord the Cid addressed him, after this wise
 he spake:
"Gramercy, lord Alfonso, I will take what thou
 hast given.
I will utter forth for this my thanks unto our
 God in Heaven,
And then to thee, and to the bands that round
 about me stand."

And on his knees yet kneeling, he kissed
    Alfonso's hand;
To his feet he rose, and on the lips greeted
    him with a kiss.
The others in the presence they were well
    pleased at this.
It irked Garci Ordoñez and Alvar Diaz sore.

My lord Cid spake and uttered this saying
    furthermore.

"To our Father and Creator I offer thanks
    again,
That my lord the King his pardon he
    vouchsafed me to attain.
In the day and the night season the Lord will
    cherish me.
Thou shalt be my guest, my master, if so thy
    pleasure be."
Said the King: "Today in no way were that
    seemly in my sight.
Thou art but now come hither, but we came in
    last night.
Today, therefore, Cid Campeador, thou shalt
    remain my guest,
And on the morrow morning we shall be at
    thy behest."

My lord the Cid has kissed his hand, granting
    it should be so.
Then came the Heirs of Carrión, their

courtesy to show:
"We greet thee Cid. Thou wast brought forth
    in an hour of promise high.
And so far will we serve thee as in our power
    may lie."
"So grant it the Creator," to them the Cid
    replied.
The Cid my lord Roy Diaz, who was born in a
    good tide,
Unto the King his master was guest for that
    day's space,
Who could not let him from his sight, he held
    him in such grace.
At the Cid's beard grown so swiftly, long while
    the King did stare.
At the Cid much they marvelled, as many as
    were there.

And now the day was over, and upon them fell
    the night.
The next day in the morning the sun rose
    clear and bright.
The Cid had bidden his henchmen meat for all
    men to array.
With my lord Cid the Campeador so well
    content were they
That all were very merry, and moreover of one
    mind
That for three years together so well they had
    not dined.

The next day in the morning, when at last the
    sun outshone,
Then did Jerome the Bishop his matin song
    intone.
And when from mass they issued, all gathered
    in one place,
And the King did not tarry but began his
    speech apace:
"Hear me now, counts and nobles, and all my
    henchmen leal–
Unto my lord Cid Campeador I needst must
    make appeal.
God grant unto his profit that the thing may
    prove to be.
Dame Sol and Dame Elvíra, I ask their hands
    of thee,
That thou wilt in marriage give them to the
    Heirs of Carrión twain.
To me the match seems noble, and thereon
    there hangs much gain.
They ask them of thee. To that end I add my
    own command.
On my side and thine as many as round about
    us stand,
My henchmen and thy henchmen, let them
    therefor intercede.
Give them to us my lord the Cid. So God thee
    help and speed."
Said the Cid: "My girls to marry are hardly yet
    in state,

For their days are not many, nor are their ages
 great.
As for the Heirs of Carrión, much fame of
 them men say;
They suit well with my daughters, and for
 better e'en than they.
'Twas I begot my daughters, but thou didst
 rear the twain.
They and I for that bounty yet in thy debt
 remain.
Dame Sol and Dame Elvíra, unto thee do I
 present,
To whom thou wilt then give them and I will
 be content."

Said the King: "My thanks unto thee and to all
 the court I own."
Upon their feet got swiftly the Heirs of
 Carrión;
Of him who in good hour was born, lightly
 they kissed the hands.
Before the King Alfonso they made exchange
 of brands.

Out spake the King Alfonso like a man of
 gentle race:
"My thanks, so noble art thou, but first to God
 for grace
That for the Heirs of Carrión thou givest thy
 daughters twain.

Dame Sol and Dame Elvíra, in hand I have
    them ta'en.
To Carrión's Heirs as consorts those ladies I
    award.
I give away thy daughters as brides with thine
    accord,
May it please God that thou therewith in full
    content mayest rest.
Behold, the heirs of Carrión that wait on thy
    behest.
Let them go with thee, prithee, for I from
    hence must wend.
Three hundred marks of silver I give them to
    this end,
To spend upon the marriage or what else
    pleaseth thee,
Since within high Valencia in thy wardship
    they will be.
The sons and the daughters shall thy children
    be all four;
Whate'er shall be thy pleasure, do with them,
    Campeador."

The Cid received them from him, and the
    King's hand did kiss.
"My sovereign and my master, I think thee
    well for this.
Thou shalt give away my daughters, for I will
    not do the deed."
After the parle was over they gave pledges

and agreed
That the next day in the morning when forth
    the sun should flame,
All persons at the parley should return to
    whence they came.
Thereby both fame and honor had the lord
    Cid Campeador,
And many mules and mighty, and fair palfreys
    furthermore,
And fine and precious raiment. And to give
    gifts he began,
Whatso he would to who would take, and
    denied it to no man.
As gifts full sixty horses did the lord Cid
    present.
Whoe'er was at the parley therewith was full
    content.
Now were they fain of parting, for night was
    like to fall.

The King the Heirs of Carrión took by the
    hand withal,
In the power of the Cid Campeador he put
    them both straightway.
"Behold them here thy children; since thy
    sons-in-law are they;
From this day forth do with them as thy heart
    shall give accord.
May they serve thee as their father, and keep
    thee for their lord."

"I thank thee and accept, O King, the gift
which thou hast given.
Mayst thou be well rewarded by God who is in
heaven.

CV.

"Of thee, my liege and sovran, a boon do I
request
Since thou givest to wed my daughters in
what way likes thee best,
Choose one my girls to give away, who in thy
place shall stand,
Since thou hast them, I will never give them
o'er with mine own hand.
To the Heirs. Such satisfaction to them shall
be denied."
"Behold here Alvar Fañez," the King to him
replied,
"Take them by the hand and give them to the
heirs, even as I
Here afar off have taken them, as though I
were hard by;
And throughout all the vigil their sponsor
shalt thou be.
When again to me thou comest tell all the
truth to me."
Said Alvar Fañez: "Faith! My lord, I am content
indeed."

CVI.

To all this with due caution, know well they

have agreed.

"Ha! King, my lord Alfonso much honored, for
    a sign

Of the parley that we held here, thou shalt
    take a gift of mine.

I bring thee thirty palfreys that are trapped
    rich and well,

And thirty fleet war-horses, each with a noble
    selle.

Take them and I will kiss thy hand."

The King Alfonso spake:

"Deep in thy debt thou hast me. Thy present I
    will take

Which thou givest. The Creator and all his
    saints accord

For the kindness thou hast done me that thou
    have a fair reward.

Oh my lord Cid Roy Diaz, thou hast done me
    honor high.

Full well thou cost my service, and well
    content am I.

Mayst thou reap of me some harvest ere my
    life be at an end.

Into God's hands I give thee. From the parley
    will I wend.

Hail God in Heaven! Grant us our treaty well
    to keep."

CVII.

The Cid mounted Baviéca his charger at a

leap.

"Here before my King Alfonso I say it openly,

Who would fain go to the marriage or would
have a gift of me,

Let him come with me. His profit shall be
great, as I conceive."

Now of his lord Alfonso the lord Cid took his
leave...

His company he wished not, he departed from
him straight.

There might you see a many of knights of fair
estate

Taking leave of King Alfonso, that the while
his hands did kiss:

"Let it be now thy pleasure, and prithee grant
us this–

'Neath the Cid to great Valencia now will we
march away

To see the Heirs of Carrión upon their
wedding day,

And Dame Sol and Dame Elvíra that the Cid's
daughters be."

Therewith the King was satisfied and gave
them liberty.

And the King's bands diminished and the
Cid's increased the more.

Great company of people marched with the
Campeador.

They rode straight to Valencia ta'en when his
    star was high.
On Diégo and Ferrándo he bade them keep an
    eye.
Muño Gustióz and Per Vermudóz they had
    commandment plain—
In all my lord Cid's household were not a
    better twain
The ways of them of Carrión to discover them
    and find.
Ansuór Gonzálvez joined the Heirs who was a
    noisy hind,
Loose-tongued, and for untrustful in other
    things well known.
They showered many honors on the Heirs of
    Carrión.

Behold them in Valencia that the Cid my lord
    had ta'en.
When they looked upon the city they were
    exceeding fain.
Muño Gustióz and don Pero, to them the lord
    Cid spake:
"Straightway the Heirs of Carrión unto a
    lodging take,
But do you tarry with them, so doth my order
    run.
When entereth in the morning, when
    breaketh forth the sun,
Of Dame Sol and Dame Elvíra, their brides,

they shall have sight."

CVIII.

Then every man departed to his lodging-place
    that night.
The Cid Campeador has entered his castle
    once again.
Abode him Dame Xiména, she and her
    daughters twain.

"Campeador who in good season girt sword,
    thou hast come thy ways;
May the eyes of our faces behold thee many
    days."

"I am come, wife much honored, by the
    Creator's grace,
And sons-in-law I bring thee, whence our
    fame shall wax apace.
I have married you well, my daughters, so
    thank me for it well.

CIX.

Forthwith a-kissing of his hands his wife and
    daughters fell,
And likewise all the ladies their pleasure still
    that did.
"Thanks be to the Creator and to thee, fair-
    bearded Cid,
What thing thou cost soever, it is well done
    indeed.

In all thy days thy daughters shall never be in
    need."

"When thou givest us in marriage, great
    wealth to us shall fall."

CX.

"Wife o'mine, Dame Xiména. praise God who
    made us all.

Dame Sol and Dame Elvíra, my girls to you
    I say,

From your marriage in all honor shall we
    increase always.

But that I did not begin it, the truth now
    understand;

My lord Alfonso sought you and stately made
    demand

With such firm will, I wist not how to deny
    the thing.

And I put you both, my daughters, in the
    keeping of the King.

Know that he giveth you to wed, and that I am
    not the man."

CXI.

To make beautiful the palace, then one and all
    began.

There was displayed much arras on wall and
    pavement both,

Much purple and much samite and store of
    precious cloth.

'Twould have pleased you in that palace to
    have sat you down to eat.
And speedily together did his knights
    assembled meet.

And for the Heirs of Carrión as at that time
    they sent,
To horse they got and onward to the palace
    forth they went.
And fine is all their raiment, and stuff of
    proof likewise.
They came afoot and properly, God! In what
    lowly guise!
The Cid and all his vassals received them
    when they came.
They bowed the head before him; they bowed
    before his dame;
Straightway to take their places on a noble
    seat they strode.
Of my lord Cid all the henchmen exceeding
    wisdom showed,
His speech who in good hour was born in
    quiet they expect.

And now the noble Campeador hath risen up
    erect:
"Since such a deed is toward, why do we tarry
    here?
Come hither Alvar Fañez whom I cherish and
    hold dear.

My daughters twain, behold them, to thy hand
    I give them o'er.
Be it known so to perform it unto the King I
    swore,
To fail in our agreement is in no way mine
    intent.
To the Heirs of Carrión their brides, now with
    thine hand present;
Let them have benediction and speed the
    wedding through."

To him replied Minaya: "This will I gladly do."

The ladies rose. He gave them into Minaya's
    care.
To Carrión's Heirs, Minaya now doth his
    charge declare:
"Lo! Minaya here before you, ye brothers born
    that be!
By the hand of King Alfonso, who has laid this
    charge on me,
I give to you these ladies that are both of
    noble blood,
That to wife ye take them nobly and in fair
    guise and good."

And with a will and gladly to take their brides
    they came,
And they kissed the hands straightway of my
    lord Cid and his dame.

They came forth from the palace when all
these things were done.
And then unto Saint Mary's in haste they got
them gone.
Bishop Jerome his vestments swiftly to him
has ta'en,
And he abode the coming at the portal of the
fane.
He has given them his blessing, and chanted
mass in course.

When from the church they issued with speed
they got to horse.
They hastened from Valencia forth on the
sandy shore.
God! The Cid and his companions, how well
their arms they bore!
He who in happy hour was born, three times
hath changed his steed.
With what he saw my lord the Cid was well
content indeed,
For the two heirs of Carrión have well their
steeds bestrode.
With the ladies to Valencia then home again
they rode.
In that fair hold resplendent was the wedding
that they had.
To rear up seven quintains the Cid next
morning bade;
Before they went to dinner, were the seven

burst in twain.

Full fifteen days together at the wedding they
      remain.
The fifteen days well nigh are done;
      homeward the nobles ride.
My lord Cid don Rodrigo who was born in a
      good tide
Of the mules and the palfreys and the battle-
      chargers swift,
Of beasts alone an hundred has granted forth
      in gift,
And cloaks, fur capes, and raiment of other
      sort great store,
and bestowed wealth in money in abundance
      furthermore.
The vassals of my lord the Cid, for they had
      counselled so,
For their part bridal tokens upon the guests
      bestow.
He came by great possession whoso thereof
      was fain,
Who was at the bridal, wealthy came to
      Castile again.
Now are all these guests together about to
      ride away;
To Roy Diaz in good hour born their last
      devoirs they pay,
And likewise to the ladies, and his men of
      high descent.

My lord Cid and his vassals they left in high
    content.
They said much honor of them as was indeed
    their due.
Diégo and Ferrándo were passing merry too;
Of the Count don Gonzálvo they were the
    children twain.

And now the guests came homeward unto
    Castile again.
The Cid and his two sons-in-law in Valencia
    they stay.
There dwell the Heirs until two years have
    well-nigh passed away.
It was a mighty welcome in that city that they
    had.
The Cid and all his vassals were all exceeding
    glad.
Saint Mary and our Father, may it please them
    to consent
That the Cid and he who wrought it with the
    bridal be content.
Of this Cantar the couplets come now unto
    their end.
The Saints and the Creator preserve you and
    defend.

CANTAR III

The Affront of Corpes

CXII.

The Cid lay in Valencia with all his men
    beside;

With him the Heirs of Carrión his sons-in-law
    abide.

Upon his couch to slumber lay the good
    Campeador.

There fell a hard occasion, a thing they looked
    not for.

From his cage came forth the lion, from his
    bonds he broke away.

All men throughout the palace in mighty
    dread were they.

'Neath the arm the Campeador his men their
    mantles up have ta'en,

About his couch they gathered, and beside
    their lord remain.

As for Ferránd Gonzálvez the Heir of Carrión,

He saw no place to hide in; chamber or tower
    was none.

Beneath the seat he crouched him so mighty
    was his dread.

And Dídago Gonzálvez out through the
    doorway fled,

Crying aloud: "Wo! Carrión no more shall I

behold."
Beneath a wine-press timber he hid in fear
        untold.
Thence he brought cloak and tunic all filthy
        and forlorn.

With that he woke from slumber, who in
        happy hour was born,
And saw his good men round his couch in a
        close ring that stood.

"Now what is this my henchmen ~ What is it
        that ye would?"

"Ha, worthy lord! The lion gave us a fearful
        fright."
The Cid leaned on his elbow, on his feet he
        leaped upright.
He flung his cloak on shoulder. Straight for
        the beast he made.
The lion when he saw him, so sorely was
        afraid
That before the Cid, low cowering, to earth
        his head he bent.
My lord Cid don Rodrigo him by the neck has
        hent.
He drew him and he dragged him and within
        his cage shut fast.
As many as he held it thought it a marvel vast.

And then through the palace they returned

unto the hall,
Of his sons the Cid made question, but found
    them not at all.
Though they shouted for them loudly, none
    answered to the hail.
And when at last they found them, oh, but
    their cheeks were pale!
Such mirth as in the palace was ye never saw
    before;
But to plague them was forbidden by the lord
    Cid Campeador.
Many thought that but for cowards
    themselves the twain had shown.
Sore grieved at what befell them were the
    Heirs of Carrión.

CXIII.

While thus the affair standeth wherein they
    had such shame,
A host out of Morocco to besiege Valencia
    came.
Their camp within the Quarter Field have
    they arrayed aright.
For fifty thousand chieftains pavilions have
    they pight.
'Twas the King Búcar if perchance of him ye
    e'er heard tell.

CXIV.

The Cid and all his henchmen, it pleased them
    passing well,

For so by the lord's favor their gain should
   grow the more.
But know the Heirs of Carrión at heart were
   very sore,
For they saw of the Moriscos many and many
   a tent,
Which liked them not. The brothers forthwith
   apart they went.
"We would keep in mind our profit, nor for
   the loss have care.
And now within this battle we must needs do
   our share."
"Such a thing well may keep us from seeing
   Carrión more.
Widows will be the daughters of the good
   Campeador."

But Muñoz Gustióz hearkened how in secret
   they conferred.
To the Cid Campeador he came with the tale
   of what he heard:
"The two Heirs thy sons-in-law, their courage
   is so strong,
Because they go to battle, for Carrión they
   long.
As God cherishes and keeps them, go bid
   them have good heart,
That they in peace may tarry, nor in battle
   have a part.
But with that we shall conquer, and God shall

be our stay."

My lord Cid don Rodrigo with a smile went
   his way.
"My sons, the Heirs of Carrión. God have you
   in his care.
In your arms rest my daughters that as the
   sun are fair.
And as I yearn for battle, so of Carrión are ye
   fain.
In pleasance in Valencia to your hearts desire
   remain!,
For as for the Moriscos, them well enough I
   know,
And by grace of the Creator have courage to
   o'erthrow."

While they spoke thus, King Búcar sent word
   and commanded The Cid
to quit Valencia and go his way in peace.[1]

Otherwise Búcar would exact payment for all
   that the Cid had done
in the city. The Cid said to him who bore the
   message:

"Go thou and say to Búcar, that son of an
   enemy, that before three
days are past, I will give him all that he asks."

---

1.   At this point a lacuna occurs in the text of the poem. The prose
   passage is supplied from the *Chronicle of the Twenty Kings*, an
   emendation due to Pidal.

The next day the Cid ordered all his men to
    take up their weapons,
and marched out against the Moors. The
    Heirs of Carrión on that
occasion sought the van of him. After the Cid
    had marshalled his
men in order of battle, don Ferrándo, one of
    the Heirs, went forth
to attack a Moor who was called Aladraf. The
    Moor, when he beheld
don Ferrándo, came forward likewise to attack
    him. Thereupon the
Heir of Carrión, being overcome with fear of
    the Moor, wheeled his
horse and fled before him. Single-handed he
    dared not await the Moor's coming.

When Pero Vermudóz, who was hard by,
    beheld this, he attacked the
Moor, fought with him and slew him. Then he
    took the Moor's horse
and went in quest of the Heir who was in full
    flight.

"Don Ferrándo," he said to him, "take this
    horse and tell all men
that thou didst slay the Moor, his master. I
    will be thy witness."
And the Heir replied: "Don Pero Vermudóz, I
    thank thee greatly for what thou sayest.

"May I see that time when payment I shall
make to thee twice o'er
For all that thou deserves". The twain turned
back once more.
Don Pero there bore witness to Ferrándo's
brag and lie.
The Cid and all his vassals were gladdened
much thereby.

"If God our Father wills it, in Heaven that
doth dwell,
My sons-in-law in battle shall both acquit
them well."

So they spake. And the two armies now the
advance began.
In the Moorish host resounded of the drums
the rataplan.
It was among the Christians a marvel sore to
some,
For never had they heard it, since but newly
were they come.
On Diégo and Ferrándo greater wonder yet
did fall,
And of their free will thither they would not
have come at all.
To what he said who was brought forth in
happy hour give ear:
"Ho! now don Pero Vermudóz, who art my
nephew dear,

Dídago and Ferrándo now keep them well
    for me,
For in mine eyes my sons-in-law are dear
    exceedingly.
By God's help the Moriscos shall hold the field
    no more."

CXVI.

"In the name of every charity I tell thee,
    Campeador,
That today to be their keeper I never will
    remain.
To me they matter little – let him keep them
    who is fain.
I with my men about me against their van will
    smite;
Do thou with thine hold firmly the rearward
    of the fight.
Then canst thou aid me lightly if peril should
    arise."

Minaya Alvar Fañez came then to him
    likewise.
"Oh, Cid, give ear, and hearken, Oh faithful
    Campeador!
For surely in this battle shall God himself
    make war,
And He will make thee worthy with Him
    therein to share.
Where 'er thou deemest fitting bid us attack
    them there.

Each man must do his duty. Upon them let us
    thrust.
On God and on thy fortune now hangeth all
    our trust."
My lord Cid said: "Then prithee tarry here yet
    awhile."
Lo! don Jerome the Bishop who was armed in
    gallant style,
He stopped before the Campeador. Fair
    fortune had he aye.
"The Mass of Holy Trinity I sang for thee this
    day.
For this cause from mine own country did I
    seek thee and ensue,
Since in the slaughter of the Moor such great
    delight I knew.
And I am fain to honor both mine order and
    mine hand.
In the forefront of the battle it is my desire to
    stand.
And crosses on my pennant, and blazoned
    arms have I.
If it be God his pleasure, I am fain mine arms
    to try,
That so at last my spirit in perfect peace
    may be,
And thou mayst be, my lord the Cid, better
    content with me.
If thou cost me not this honor, from thy side I
    will retire."

The lord Cid gave him answer: "I am pleased
    with thy desire.
Of the Moors go make a trial, lo, where they
    are in sight.
From hence we shall behold it, how the Abbot
    fights the fight."

CXVII.
And don Jerome the Bishop went spurring
    thence away.
'Gainst the end of the encampment he guided
    forth the fray.
By his good hap and God's mercy who ever
    loved him well,
At the first stroke he delivered two Moors
    before him fell.
When in twain his lance was broken, he set
    hand upon the blade.
Well was he tried. And Name of God! What a
    fair fight he made!
Two with the lance, and with the sword five
    of the foe he slew.
The Moors are very many. Around him close
    they drew,
They did not pierce his armour, though they
    laid on strokes of power.

His eyes beheld the Bishop, who was born in
    happy hour,
He caught his shield, the battle-spear he laid
    it low along,

He spurred Baviéca the well-paced steed and
    strong,
He went to smite against them with all his
    soul and heart.
The foremost ranks of battle did the lord Cid
    dispart:
Of the Moors he struck down seven, and five
    of them hath slain.
God was well pleased, the battle it was
    granted him to gain.
My lord Cid and his henchmen in hot pursuit
    they went.
There had you seen the stakes uptorn and
    may a tent-rope rent,
And all the ten-poles falling that were
    wrought so rich and brave.
From the tents, my lord Cid's vassals King
    Búcar's henchmen drave.

CXVIII.

Out of the tents they drave them; on them in
    pursuit they flew.
Many arms and many a hauberk, had you seen
    there cloven through,
And many a head well helmed in the battle
    fallen low,
And many a steed masterless that galloped to
    and fro.
For seven miles together they followed up the
    flight.

As he followed, on King Búcar the Cid my lord
    did light:
"Turn hither, Búcar. thou hast come from the
    land over sea.
The Cid whose beard is mighty thou shalt
    meet with presently.
Let us greet, and in fast friendship let each to
    each be bound."
To the Cid answered Búcar: "Such a friendship
    God confound.
A sword in hand thou bearest, and I see thee
    spur amain,
Seemeth well that thou upon me to try that
    blade art fain.
If my horse keep from stumbling and falleth
    not with me.
Thou shalt not overtake me till we ride into
    the sea."
My lord Cid answered: "With the truth that
    word no faith shall keep."
A good steed had Búcar that sprang off great
    leap on leap.
But the Cid's Baviéca upon him fast did gain.
Three fathoms from the water was Búcar
    overtaken.
He has lifted up Coláda. A great stroke did he
    smite.
The carbuncles upon his helm he has smitten
    through forthright.
He cut straight through the helmet, all else in

twain he crave,
And slashing to the girdle of the King came
down the glaive.
Búcar the King from oversea the Cid hath
overthrown.
Well worth a thousand golden marks was the
great sword Tizón,
That he took there. 'Twas a victory most
marvelous and great.
Here my lord Cid got honor and all that on
him wait.

CXIX.
And now with all that booty, homeward again
they wheeled.
And be it known that steadfastly they
plundered all the field.
With him who in good hour was born to the
fonts they came once more;
My lord the Cid Roy Diaz, the famous
Campeador,
With two swords he greatly cherished
through the carnage swiftly passed.
O'er his brow his cap was wrinkled, back was
his mail-hood cast,
And but a little ruffled was the cap upon his
hair.
On every side his henchmen came thronging
to him there.
My lord the Cid saw somewhat and was well

pleased thereby,
For he looked forth before him lifting up his
    eyes on high.
And Diégo and Ferrándo he beheld, that near
    him drew.
Of the Count don Gonzalvo the children were
    the two.
My lord the Cid smiled beautifully, for a glad
    man was he.

"Are ye come here, my sons-in-law? Ye are both
    sons to me.
I know that with the fighting ye are right well
    content.
To Carrión fair tidings that concern you shall
    be sent,
How by us the King Búcar unto defeat was
    thrust.
As sure as unto the Lord God and all his
    saints I trust,
With the rout of the foeman shall we all we be
    satisfied.
Minaya Alvar Fañez came now unto his side.
Hacked with the swords was all the shield that
    at his neck he wore.
The strokes of many lances had scarred it
    furthermore.
They that those strokes had stricken, had
    reaped therefrom no gain.
Down the blood streamed from his elbows.

More than twenty had he slain.
"To God and to the Father on High now
    praises be,
And Cid who in good hour wast born so
    likewise unto thee.
Thou slewest the King Búcar, and we have won
    the day.
To thee and to thy vassals belongeth all the
    prey.
And as for thy two sons-in-law they have been
    proved aright,
Who got their fill of Moorish war upon the
    field of fight."

Said my lord Cid in answer, "I therefore am
    right glad.
Since they are proved, hereafter in esteem
    shall they be had."

In honesty he said it, but a jest the thing they
    thought.
The prey unto Valencia they gathered and
    they brough't.
My lord the Cid was merry and his vassals
    with him there.
Six hundred marks of silver were allotted to
    his share.

The sons-in-law of my lord Cid, when they had
    ta'en away
Their war-prize, when the booty safe in their

hand had they,
Took care that no decrease thereof should in
    their time be made.
In the city of Valencia they were splendidly
    arrayed,
Feeding well, and wearing noble cloaks and
    gallant capes of fur.
The Cid and all his henchmen exceeding glad
    they were.

CXX.

'Twas a great day in the palace of the Cid
    Campeador,
When he had slain King Búcar and they won
    the field of war.
He raised his hand, he plucked his beard: "To
    Christ now glory be,
Who is the Lord of all the Earth, for my desire
    I see,
That with me in the battle my two sons
    should front the foe.
Of them most noble tidings to Carrión shall
    go:
How they are greatly honored, and what
    renown they gain."

CXXI.

It was a mighty booty that the Cid his host
    had taken.
Part is their own. In safety they kept the rest

aside.

My lord the Cid gave orders who was born in a
    good tide,

That to all men of that conquest his true
    share they should allot,

And that the fifth of my lord Cid should
    nowise be forgot.

And all men did according, being prudent one
    and all.

For his fifth, six hundred horses to my lord
    Cid did fall,

And there were many camels and, moreover,
    mules as well.

Of them there were so many, that their
    number none might tell.

CXXII.

All of this prey was captured by the great
    Campeador:

"Now unto God be glory who is Lord the
    whole world o'er.

Before I was in poverty who have grown rich
    and great,

For now I have possessions, gold, honor, and
    estate;

And the two Heirs of Carrión my sons-in-law
    are they.

And since it is God's pleasure I win in every
    fray;

And the Moors and the Christians they have

great dread of me.
And over in Morocco, where many mosques
there be,
Where all men are in terror lest upon them I
descend
On some fine night. That venture in no way I
intend –
I shall not go to seek them. In Valencia I shall
stay.
By God's aid, to me their tribute they shall
render up and pay.
To me or unto whom I will, they shall pay the
money down."

Very great was the rejoicing in Valencia the
town
That rose in all the levies of the Cid
Campeador,
That God's will hath vouchsafed them to
triumph in the war.
Likewise of both his sons-in-law excelling was
the mirth,
For each of them won booty five thousand
marks in worth.
Themselves they deem right wealthy, those
Heirs of Carrión twain.

And they with all the others to the palace
came again.
With my lord the Cid the Bishop don Jerome

standeth here.

And the good Alvar Fañez, the fighting
    cavalier.

Of the Campeador his household are many
    others by.

When the heirs of Carrión entered, they were
    given greeting high.

By Minaya for the sake of my lord Cid
    Campeador:

"Come, brothers, by your presence now are we
    honored more."

When they were come the Campeador was
    merry of his cheer:

"Lo! now behold, my sons-in-law, my faithful
    wife and dear,

With Dame Sol and Dame Elvíra that are my
    daughters twain,

Now nobly may they serve you and nobly
    entertain.

Now glory to Saint Mary, Mother of our Lord!
    God's name!

You are like from these your marriages to win
    abundant fame.

Unto the land of Carrión fair tidings shall be
    sped."

CXXIII.

Out spake the Heir Ferrándo when all the
    word was said:

"Glory to the Creator, and, noble Cid, to thee.

We have so many riches that numberless
    they be.
Through you we have much honor, and we
    have fought for you;
We conquered the Moriscos in the battle, and
    we slew
King Búcar, proven traitor, so pray you have a
    care
Now for some other matter; well marcheth
    our affair."

My lord the Cid his henchmen spake smiling
    round about
Of whoso fought most fiercely or best
    pursued the rout.

But Diégo and Ferrándo mid such men they
    did not find.
And now in all the japing the henchmen had
    designed
Both day and night together they mocked
    sore the Heirs again.
A very evil counsel together took the twain.
Verily they are brothers, forthwith apart they
    turn
To the thing that they have spoken, let us
    have no concern.
"Let us return to Carrión. Here overlong we
    wait.
The riches we have gathered are excellent and

great.

We cannot hope to spend them in the
    mountance of our lives.

CXXIV.

"Now of the Cid the Campeador let us demand
    our wives.

Let us say that we will bear them to the lands
    of Carrión.

The place where they are heiresses shall unto
    them be shown.

We shall take them from Valencia, from the
    Campeador his reach.

And then upon the journey we shall work our
    will on each,

Ere the matter of the lion for a sore reproach
    and scorn

They turn to our discomfort who are heirs of
    Carrión born.

We shall bear with us of treasure nigh
    priceless a fair stock.

Of the daughters of the Campeador we two
    shall make our mock.

We shall be rich men always who possess such
    valiant things,

And fit to marry daughters of emperors or
    kings,

Who art the Counts of Carrión by virtue of
    our birth.

The Campeador his daughters we shall mock

at in our mirth.
Ere the matter of the lion they throw at us in
     disdain."

When this they had decided the two returned
     again.
Outspoke Ferránd Golzalvez for silence in the
     Court:

"Cid Campeador, so may our God abide thy
     strong support,
May it please Dame Xiména, but first seem
     good to thee,
And Minaya Alvar Fañez and all men here
     that be
Give us our wives. By marriage are they ours
     in very deed.
Unto our lands in Carrión those ladies we will
     lead.
With the dower-lands to enfeoff them that we
     gave for bridal right
Of the lands of our possession, thy daughters
     shall have sight,
And those wherein the children to be born to
     us shall share."

The Cid my lord the Campeador scented no
     insult there:
"I shall give you my daughters and of my
     wealth dispone.
Ye gave them glebe of dowry in the lands of

Carrión,

Three thousands marks of dower shall to my
girls belong.

I will give mules and palfreys both excellent
and strong,

And great steeds of battle swift and of mighty
thew,

And cloth and silken garments with the gold
woven through.

Coláda and Tizón the swords I will give to you
likewise

Full well ye know I got them in very gallant
guise.

My sons ye are, for to you do I give my
daughters two.

My very heart's blood thither ye carry home
with you.

In León and in Galicia and Castile let all men
hear

How I sent forth my sons-in-law with such
abundant gear.

And serve you well my daughters, your
wedded wives that be.

An' you serve them well rich guerdon ye shall
obtain of me."

To this the heirs of Carrión their full assent
made plain.

The daughters of the Campeador were given
them and taken,

And they began receiving as the Cid's orders

went.
When of all their heart's desire they were at
    last content,
Then Carrión's heirs commanded that the
    packs be loaded straight,

Through Valencia the city was the press of
    business great,
And all have taken weapons and all men gallop
    strong,
For they must forth the daughters of the Cid
    to speed along
Unto the lands of Carrión. To mount all men
    prepare,
Farewell all men are saying. But the two
    sisters there,
Dame Sol and Dame Elvíra, kneeled to the Cid
    Campeador:
"A boon, so may God keep thee, O father, we
    implore.

Thou begottest us. Our mother she brought
    us forth in pain.
Our liege-lord and our lady, here do ye stand
    ye twain.
Now to the lands of Carrión to send us is your
    will;
It is our bounden duty thy commandment to
    fulfil.
And so we two together ask but this boon of

thee,
That in the lands of Carrión thy tidings still
    may be."
My lord the Cid has clasped them, and he has
    kissed the twain.

CXXV.

This hath he done. Their mother hath
    doubled it again.
"Go, daughters! the Creator of you henceforth
    have care
Mine and your father's blessing you still with
    you shall bear.
Go forth where you are dowered in Carrión to
    dwell.
I have, after my thinking, married you passing
    well."
The hands of their father and their mother
    kissed the two.
Blessing and benediction they gave to them
    anew.

My lord Cid and the others have fettled them
    to ride,
With armor and with horses and caparisons of
    pride.
From Valencia the splendid were the Heirs
    departing then.
They took leave of the ladies and all their
    bands of men.

Through the meadow of Valencia forth under
    arms they went.
The Cid and all his armies were very well
    content.
He who in good hour belted brand in signs
    had seen it plain
That these marriages in no way should stand
    without a stain.
But since the twain are married, he may not
    repent him now.

CXXVI.
"My nephew Felez Múñoz, I prithee where art
    thou?
Thou art my daughters' cousin in thy soul and
    in thine heart.
With them even unto Carrión I command thee
    to depart.
Thou shalt see what lands for dower to my
    girls are given o'er,
And shalt come again with tidings unto the
    Campeador."

Quoth Felez Múñoz: "Heart and soul that duty
    pleases me."
Minaya Alvar Fañez before the Cid came he:
"Back to the town of Valencia, Oh Cid, now let
    us go;
For if our God and Father the Creator's will
    be so,
To Carrión's lands thy daughters to visit we

shall wend.

Dame Sol and Dame Elvíra, to God do we
commend.

Such things may you accomplish as will make
us glad and fain."

The sons-in-law gave answer: "Now that may
God ordain."

They lamented much at parting. Daughters
and sire wept sore,

So also wept the cavaliers of the Cid
Campeador.

"Thou, cousin, Felez Múñoz, now hark to this
aright.

Thou shalt go by Molína, and there shalt lie
one night,

And greet fair the Morisco Avengalvón my
friend;

That he may most fair reception to my sons-
in-law extend.

Tell him I send my daughters to the lands of
Carrión,

In all their needs his courtesy as beseemeth
shall be shown.

Let him ward them to Medína for the love he
beareth me.

For all that he cloth for them I will give him a
rich fee."

They parted then, as when the nail out of the

flesh is torn.

He turned back to Valencia who in happy hour
    was born.
And now the Heirs of Carrión have fettled
    them to fare.
Saint Mary of Alvarrazín, their halting-place
    was there.

From thence the Heirs of Carrión plied
    furiously the spur.
Ho! in Molína with the Moor Avengalvón they
    were.
The Morisco when he heard it in his heart was
    well content,
And forth with great rejoicings to welcome
    them he went.
Ah, God! how well he served them in what e
    'er their joy might be!
The next day in the morning to horse with
    them got he.
He bade two hundred horsemen for escort
    forth to ride.
They crossed the mountains of Luzón (so are
    they signified),
And the Vale of Arbujuélo to the Jalón they
    came.
The place where they found lodging, Ansaréra
    is its name.
Unto the daughters of the Cid, the Moor fair

presents gave,
And to either Heir of Carrión beside a charger
    brave.
For the love he bore the Campeador, all this
    for them he wrought.

They looked upon the riches that the Moor
    with him had brought
And then together treason did the brothers
    twain concert.
"Since the daughters of the Campeador we
    shortly shall desert,
If but we might do unto death Aengalvon the
    Moor,
The treasure he possesses for ourselves we
    should secure
Safe as our wealth in Carrión those goods we
    will maintain.
And ne'er will the Cid Campeador avenge on
    us the stain."
While they of Carrión this shame complotted
    each with each,
In the midst a Moor o'erheard them, that
    could of Latin speech.
He kept no secret. With it to Avengalvón he
    ran:
"Thou art my lord. Be wary of these persons,
    Castellan.
I heard the heirs of Carrión that plotted death
    for thee."

CXXVII.

This same Avengalvón the Moor, a gallant man
    was he

He got straightway on horseback with
    servitors ten score.

He brandished high his weapons, he came the
    Heirs before.

And the two Heirs with what he said but little
    pleased they are:

"If for his sake I forebore not, my lord Cid of
    Bivár,

I would do such deeds upon you as through all
    the world should ring,

And then to the true Campeador his
    daughters would I bring.

And unto Carrión never should you enter
    from that day.

CXXVIII.

What I have done against you, ho! Heirs of
    Carrión, say,

For without guile I served you, and lo, my
    death ye plot.

For wicked men and traitors I will leave you
    on the spot.

Dame Sol and Dame Elvíra with your good
    leave I go;

For of these men of Carrión I rate the fame
    but low.

God will it and command it, who is Lord of all

the Earth.
That the Campeador hereafter of this match
    have joy and mirth."
That thing the Moor has told them, and back
    he turned him there.
When he crossed over thee Jalón, weapon he
    waved in air.
He returned unto Molína like a man of
    prudent heart.

And now from Ansaréra did Carrión's Heirs
    depart;
And they began thereafter to travel day and
    night.
And they let Atiénza on the left, a craggy
    height.
The forest of Miédes, now have they
    overpassed,
And on through Montes Claros they pricked
    forward spurring fast.
And then passed Griza on the left that Alamos
    did found.
There be the caves where Elpha he
    imprisoned underground.
And they left San Estévan, on their right that
    lay afar.
Within the woods of Corpes, the Heirs of
    Carrión are.
And high the hills are wooded, to the clouds
    the branches sweep,

And savage are the creatures that roundabout
  them creep;
And there upon a bower with a clear spring
  they light
And there the Heirs of Carrión bade that their
  tent be pight.
There with their men about them, that night
  they lay at rest.
With their wives clasped to their bosom their
  affection they protest,
But ill the twain fulfilled it, when the dawn
  came up the East.
They bade put goods a plenty on the back of
  every beast.
Where they at night found lodging, now have
  they struck the tent.
The people of their household far on before
  them went.
Of the two Heirs of Carrión so the
  commandment ran,
That none behind should linger, a woman or a
  man.
But Dame Sol and Dame Elvíra their wives
  shall tarry still,
With whom it is their pleasure to dally to
  their fill.

The others have departed. They four are left
  alone.
Great evil had been plotted by the Heirs of

Carrión.

"Dame Sol and Dame Elvíra, ye may take this
    for true:

Here in the desert wildwood shall a mock be
    made of you.

Today is our departure, we will leave you here
    behind.

And in the lands of Carrión no portion shall
    you find.

Let them hasten with these tidings to the Cid
    Campeador.

Thus, the matter of the lion, we avenge
    ourselves therefor."

Their furs and their mantles, from the ladies
    they have whipped.

In their shifts and their tunics they left the
    ladies stripped.

With spur on heel before them those wicked
    traitors stand,

And saddle-girths both stout and strong they
    have taken in the hand.

When the ladies had beheld it, then out spake
    Sol the dame:

"Don Diégo, don Ferrándo, we beeech you in
    God's name.

You have two swords about you, that for
    strength and edge are known.

And one they call Coláda, the other is Tizón.
    Strike off our heads together, and martyrs

we shall die.
The Moriscos and the Christians against this
    deed shall cry.
It stands not with our deserving that we
    should suffer thus.
So evil an example, then do not make of us.
Unto our own abasement, if you scourge us,
    you consent,
That men will bring against you in parle and
    parliament."

Naught profits it the ladies, however hard
    they pray.
And now the Heirs of Carrión upon them 'gan
    to lay.
With the buckled girths they scourged them
    in fashion unbeseen,
And exceeding was their anguish from the
    sharp spurs and keen.
They rent the shifts and wounded the bodies
    of the two,
And forth upon the tunics the clear blood
    trickled through.
In their very hearts the ladies have felt that
    agony.
What a fair fortune were it, if God's will it
    might be,
Had then appeared before them the Cid the
    Campeador.

Powerless were the ladies, and the brothers
    scourged them sore.
Their shifts and their sullies throughout the
    blood did stain.
Of scourging the two ladies wearied the
    brothers twain,

Which man should smite most fiercely they
    had vied each with each.
Dame Sol and Dame Elvíra had no longer
    power of speech.
Within the wood of Corpes for dead they left
    the pair.

CXXIX.
Their cloaks and furs of ermine along with
    them they bare,
In their shifts and tunics, fainting, they left
    them there behind,
A prey to every wild-fowl and beast of savage
    kind.

Know you, for dead, not living, they left them
    in such cheer.
Good hap it were if now the Cid, Roy Diaz,
    should appear.

CXXX.
The Heirs of Carrión for dead have left them
    thus arrayed,
For the one dame to the other, could give no

sort of aid.
They sang each other's praises as they
    journeyed through the wood:
"For the question of our marriage we have
    made our vengeance good.
Unbesought, to be our lemans we should not
    take that pair,
Because as wedded consorts for our arms
    unfit they were.
For the insult of the lion vengeance shall thus
    be ta'en."

CXXXI.

They sang each other's praises, the Heirs of
    Carrión twain.
But now of Felez Múñoz will I tell the tale
    once more.
Even he that was nephew to the Cid
    Campeador.
They had bidden him ride onward, but he was
    not well content.
And his heart smote within him as along the
    road he went.
Straightway from all the others' a space did
    he withdraw.
There Felez Múñoz entered into a thick-
    grown straw,
Till the coming of his cousins should be plain
    to be perceived
Or what the Heirs of Carrión as at that time

achieved.

And he beheld them coming, and heard them
    say their say,

But they did not espy him, nor thought of him
    had they.

Be it known death he had not scaped, had they
    on him laid eye.

And the two Heirs rode onward, pricking fast
    the spur they ply.

On their trail Felez Múñoz has turned him
    back again.

He came upon his cousins. In a swoon lay the
    twain.

And crying "Oh my cousins!" straightway did
    he alight.

By the reins the horse he tethered, and went
    to them forthright.

"Dame Sol and Dame Elvíra, cousins of mine
    that be,

The two Heirs of Carrión have borne them
    dastardly.

Please God that for this dealing they may get
    a shameful gain."

And straightway he bestirred him to life to
    bring the twain.

Deep was their swoon. Of utterance all power
    they had forlorn.

Of his heart the very fabric thereby in twain
    was torn.

"Oh my cousins Dame Elvíra and Dame Sol,"
 he cried and spake,
"For the love of the Creator, my cousins twain,
 awake,
While yet the day endureth, ere falls the
 evening-hour,
Lest in the wood our bodies the savage beast
 devour."

In Dame Sol and Dame Elvíra fresh life began
 to rise;
And they looked on Felez Múñoz when at last
 they opened their eyes:
"For the love of God my cousins, now be of
 courage stout.
From the time the Heirs of Carrión shall miss
 me from their rout,
With utmost speed thereafter will they hunt
 me low and high.
And if God will not help us, in this place we
 then must die."
To him out spoke the Lady Sol in bitter agony:
"If the Campeador, our father, deserveth well
 of thee,
My cousin give us water, so may God help thee
 too."
A hat had Felez Múñoz, from Valencia, fine
 and new,
Therein he caught the water, and to his
 cousins bore.

To drink their fill he gave them, for they were
    stricken sore.
Till they rose up, most earnestly he begged
    them and implored.
He comforts them and heartens them until
    they are restored.
He took the two and quickly set them a-horse
    again.
He wrapped them in his mantle. He took the
    charger's rein
And sped them on, and through Corpes Wood
    they took their way.
They issued from the forest between the
    night and day.
The waters of Duéro they at the last attain.
At Dame Urráca's tower he left behind the
    twain,
And then unto Saint Stephen's did Felez
    Múñoz fare.
He found Diégo Tellez, Alvar Fañez' vassal,
    there.
When he had heard those tidings on his heart
    great sorrow fell.
And he took beasts of burden and garments
    that excel.
Dame Sol and Dame Elvíra to welcome did
    he go.
He lodged them in Saint Stephen's. Great
    honor did he show
Those ladies. In Saint Stephen's very gentle

are the men,
When they had heard the tidings their hearts
    were sorry then.
To the Cid's daughters tribute of plenteous
    fare they yield.
In that place the ladies tarried, till the time
    when they were healed.

Loud they sang each other's praises, those
    Heirs of Carrión,
And of their deeds the tidings through all
    these lands were known.
Of the good King don Alfonso the heart for
    grief was torn.
To Valencia the city now are the tidings
    borne.
To my lord Cid the Campeador that message
    when they brought,
Thereon for a full hour's space, he pondered
    and he thought.
His hand he has uplifted and gripped his
    beard amain:
"Now unto Christ be glory who o'er all the
    earth doth reign.
Since thus sought they of Carrión to keep
    mine honor whole.
Now by this beard that never was plucked by
    living soul,
Thereby the Heirs of Carrión no pleasure
    shall they gain.

As for the dames my daughters, I shall marry
  well the twain.

The Cid and all his courtiers were sorry
  grievously,
Heart and soul Alvar Fañez a sad man was he.
Minaya with Per Vermudóz straightway the
  steed bestrode,
And good Martin Antolínez in Burgos that
  abode,
With ten score horse that to that end the Cid
  set in array.
Most earnestly he charged them to ride both
  night and day,
And to the town Valencia his daughters twain
  to bring.
About their lord's commandment there was
  no tarrying.
Swiftly they got on horseback and rode both
  day and night.
Into Gormaz they entered, a strong place of
  might.
In sooth one night they lodged there. To Saint
  Stephen's tidings flew
That Minaya was come thither to bring home
  his cousins two.
The dwellers in Saint Stephen's, as becomes
  the true and brave,
To Minaya and his henchmen a noble welcome
  gave,

And for tribute to Minaya brought that night
　　of cheer good store.
He desired not to accept it, but he thanked
　　them well therefor;
"Thanks, stout men of Saint Stephen's, for ye
　　bear you wise and well.
For the honor that ye did us, for the thing
　　that us befell,
Where bides the Cid the Campeador he gives
　　true thanks to you,
As I do here. May God on high give you your
　　payment due."

Therewith they thanked him greatly, with
　　him were all content
Then swiftly to their lodging to rest that
　　night they went.
Where bode his kin, Minaya to see them went
　　his ways.
Dame Sol and Dame Elvíra upon him fixed
　　their gaze:
"So heartily we thank thee, as our eyes on God
　　were set,
And prithee thank Him for it, since we are
　　living yet.
In the days of ease thereafter, in Valencia
　　when we dwell,
The tale of our affliction, we shall have
　　strength to tell.

CXXXII.

The dames and Alvar Fañez, the tears flowed
    from their eyes.
Per Vermudóz because of them was sorely
    grieved likewise.
"Dame Sol and Dame Elvíra, be not down-
    hearted still,
Since you are well and living and without
    other ill.
Ye have lost a good marriage, better matches
    shall ye make.
Oh may we soon behold the day when
    vengeance we shall take!"
So all that night they lay there keeping a
    merry tide.

The next day in the morning they fettled
    them to ride.
The people of Saint Stephen's their party
    escort bore,
With every sort of solace e'en to Riodamor.
There they took leave, and got them in stead
    to travel back.
Minaya and the ladies rode forward on the
    track;
They have passed Alcoceva. On the right
    Gormaz left they.
They have come o'er the river in the place
    called Vadorrey,
And in the town Berlanga their lodging have

they made.
The next day in the morning set forth the
    cavalcade.
In the place called Medína their shelter have
    they sought.
From Medína to Molína on the next day were
    they brought.
And there the Moor Avengalvón was pleased
    in heart thereby.
Forth with good will he issued to give them
    welcome high,
For my lord Cid's love a supper he gave them
    rich and great.
Thence on unto Valencia they have departed
    straight.
When to him who in good honor was born the
    news of it was sent,
Swiftly he got on horseback, and forth to
    greet them went.
As he rode he brandished weapons; very joyful
    was his face.
My lord the Cid came forward his daughters
    to embrace.
And after he had kissed them he smiled upon
    the two:
"Are ye then come my daughters? 'Gainst ill
    God succor you.
This marriage I accepted, daring not say
    otherwise.
May the Creator grant it, who dwelleth in the

skies,
That you with better husbands hereafter I
may see.
God! on my sons of Carrión grant me avenged
to be.
"The hands of their father to kiss, the two
bent down.
And under arms they hastened and came into
the town.
Their mother Dame Xiména with them good
cheer she made.
And he who in good hour was born, he tarried
not nor stayed,
But there unto his comrades so privily he
spake:
To King Alfonso of Castile those tidings shall
they take.

CXXXIII.

"Where art thou, Muño Gustióz, vassal of fair
report
In a good time I cherished and reared thee in
my court.
To King Alfonso in Castile these tidings do
thou take.
His hands with heart and spirit do thou kiss
them for my sake–
I am known for his vassal, he for my lord is
known–
At the dishonor done me by the heirs of

Carrión
Shall the good King be troubled in his soul
    and in his heart.
He gave to wed my daughters, therein I had
    no part.
Since my girls they have deserted with great
    dishonor thus,
If they have put an insult by that action
    upon us,
The great part and the little, my lord's is all
    the scorn.
My possessions, which are mighty, off with
    them have they borne,
This and the other insult well may make me
    ill content.
Bring them to parley with me in assize or
    parliament,
So that I may have justice on the heirs of
    Carrión,
For in my heart the anguish exceeding great
    is grown."
Thereupon Muño Gustióz swiftly the steed
    bestrode.
To wait upon his pleasure two horsemen with
    him rode,
And with him were esquires that of his
    household were.
They departed from Valencia as fast as they
    could spur,
They gave themselves no respite either by

night or noon.
And the King don Alfonso he found at
    Sahagún.
Of Castile is he the ruler, of León
    furthermore.
And likewise of Asturias, yea, to San Salvador.
As far as Santiago for lord paramount is he
    known.
The counts throughout Galicia him for their
    sovereign own.
As soon as Muño Gustióz got down from
    horseback there,
Before the Saints he kneeled him, and to God
    he made his prayer.
Where the court was in the palace
    straightway his steps he bent.
The horsemen two that served him as their
    lord beside him went.
As soon as they had entered amid the royal
    train
The King saw them and knew lightly Muño
    Gustióz again.
The King rose up and nobly he welcomed him
    and well.
before the King Alfonso on bended knee he
    fell.
The King's feet, Muño Gustióz, that wight,
    has kissed withal:
"A boon, King, thee the sovereign of kingdoms
    broad they call.

The Campeador, he kisses so well thy feet and
    hands;
Thou art his lord; thy vassal as at all times he
    stands.
To Carrión's Heirs his daughters were given to
    wed by thee.
It was a glorious marriage for it was thy
    decree.
The honor that befell us is to thee already
    known,
What flout was put upon us by the Heirs of
    Carrión.
Fiercely they scourged the daughters of the
    Cid Campeador.
Naked, in great dishonor and from the
    scourging sore,
In Corpes Wood unguarded they cast the
    dames away,
Unto the savage creatures and the forest-fowl
    a prey,
And lo! now to Valencia his daughters are
    restored.
For this thy hand he kisses as a vassal to his
    lord,
That thou bring them to confront him in
    assize or parliament.
He holds himself dishonored, but fouler art
    thou shent.
And King, sore should it grieve thee, and he
    prays, for wise art thou,

That my lord Cid may have justice on the
    Heirs of Carrión now."
The king long while was silent, pondering
    thereon apart:
"The truth will I say to thee. It grieves me to
    the heart.
So hast thou, Muño Gustióz, herein a true
    thing said,
For to Carrión's Heirs, his daughters I gave
    indeed to wed.
For good I did it, deeming that there his
    vantage lay.
But would now that that marriage had ne'er
    been made today.
My lord the Cid and I myself, sore grieved at
    heart are we.
I must help him unto justice, so God my savior
    be.
Though I would not at this season, I must do
    even so.
And now through all my Kingdom forth shall
    mine heralds go,
For in Toledo city a court shall they proclaim,
So that counts may come and nobles that be
    of lesser name.
The Heirs of Carrión thither I will summon
    furthermore;
And there shall they give justice to my lord
    Cid Campeador.

Yet while I can prevent it, he shall have no
    cause to mourn.

CXXXIV.

"And say unto the Campeador, who in good
    hour was born,

That he may with his vassals for these seven
    weeks prepare

To come unto Toledo. That term I grant him
    fair.

I will hold these assizes since the Cid to me is
    dear.

Greet them all for me fairly, let them be of
    joyful cheer.

For what befell, of honor they yet shall have
    no lack."

His leave ta'en, Muño Gustióz to my lord Cid
    turned back.

Since he had undertaken that the charge on
    him should fall,

Alfonso the Castilian delayed it not at all.

To León and Santiago he sent letters without
    fail,

And unto the Galicians, and the men of
    Portingale.

Tidings to them in Carrión and in Castile they
    bring,

Of a Court held in Toledo by the much
    honored King,

And that there they should be gathered when

seven weeks should end.

Who stayed at home, true vassalage no longer
could pretend.

And all men so determined throughout his
breadth of lands

Not to fail in the fulfillment of the King's
high commands.

CXXXV.

Now are the Heirs of Carrión troubled by the
report

That the King within Toledo was about to
hold his court.

They fear my lord Cid Campeador will have
his part therein,

And they took counsel, seeing that they were
near of kin.

The King for dispensation to stay from court
they prayed.

Said the King:

"I will not do it, as God shall stand mine aid.

For my lord Cid the Campeador that place
shall come unto,

And you shall do him justice for he makes
complaint of you.

Who refuses, or denies it to come unto mine
assize,

Let him quit my realm. The fellow finds no
favor in mine eyes."

And now the Heirs of Carrión saw that it must

be done.

Since they are very near of kin, counsel they
    took thereon.
Count García that to ruin the Cid sought
    evermore,
My lord the Cid's arch-foeman, share in these
    matters bore.
This man has given counsel to the Heirs of
    Carrión twain.
Time came: to the assizes to hasten they were
    fain.
Thither among the foremost doth good King
    Alfonso go,
With him the Count don Henry, and Count
    don Remónd also–
For the sire of the most noble the Emperor
    was he known.
There came the Count don Froíla and the
    Count don Birbón.
Out of his realm came many of wise hearts
    and leal
All the best men were gathered of the
    kingdom of Castile.
And there with Crespo de Grañón, Count don
    García came
And he who ruled in Oca–Alvar Diaz was his
    name.
With Gonzalvo Ansuórez, Ansuór Gonzálvez
    stood.

Know ye well with them was Pero of the
    Ansuórez blood.
Diégo and Ferrándo both to the place resort,
And with them a great company that they had
    brought to Court.
Upon my lord Cid Campeador 'tis their intent
    to fall.

Unto the place they gather from every side
    and all.
But he who in good hour was born, not yet
    hath he drawn nigh.
Because so long he tarries is the king
    displeased thereby.
My lord the Cid the Campeador is come on
    the fifth day.
He has sent Alvar Fañez ahead of his array,
That he might kiss the King his hands that is
    his lord of right,
The King might know it surely, he would be at
    hand that night.
Now when the King had heard it, his heart
    was glad indeed.
With companies most mighty the King leaped
    on the steed,
And him who in good hour was born he went
    to welcome there.
Came the Cid and all his henchmen equipped
    exceeding fair.
Oh! noble troops that follow a captain of such

might!

When good King don Alfonso of my lord the
  Cid got sight,

My lord the Cid, the Campeador, cast himself
  on the sward.

Himself he thus could humble and do honor
  to his lord.

When the King saw he tarried not.
"Saint Isidore to speed!

This day so shalt thou never. Mount, Cid,
  upon the steed!

If not, so ends my pleasure. Let us greet on
  either part

With heart and soul. What grieveth thee hath
  hurt me to the heart.

God ordereth that by thee the court this day
  shall honored be."

My lord Cid, the true Campeador, to this
  "Amen" said he.

He kissed his hand and fairly gave him
  greeting then:

"To God now thanks be given, that I see thee,
  lord, again.

To thee I bow, so also to Count don Remónd I
  bow,

To Count Henry and to all men that are in
  presence now.

God save our friends and foremost, sire, may
  he cherish thee.

My wife the Dame Xiména – a worthy dame is

she –

Kisses thy hands. My daughters, the twain do
    so as well,

That so thou mayst have pity for the ill thing
    that befell."

"Verily, so God help me," answered the King
    thereto.

CXXXVI.

Then homeward to Toledo, the King returned
    anew.

Unfain to cross the Tagus was my lord Cid
    that night:

"A boon, King. The Creator, may he shield thee
    in His might!

Oh sire, do thou get ready to enter in the
    town.

In San Serván my henchman and I will lay us
    down,

For hither in the night-tide shall come those
    bands of mine;

And I will keep my vigil here by the holy
    shrine.

I will come to town tomorrow at the breaking
    of the day,

And, ere I eat my dinner, to court will take my
    way."

To him the King gave answer: "Surely, I am
    content."

Then the King don Alfonso into Toledo went.

My lord the Cid Roy Diaz lieth in San Serván.
To make candles and to set them on the
    shrine, his order ran.
To watch that sanctuary was gladness to his
    heart,
As he prayed to the Creator and spake to him
    apart.
Minaya, and as many as were gathered of good
    fame
Were in accord together when at length the
    morning came.

CXXXVII.

Matins and prime they sang there till the
    dawn had begun,
Before the sun had risen the mass was o'er
    and done.
With rich and timely offering that chapel they
    endow.
"Minaya Alvar Fañez – my strongest arm art
    thou –
Thyself shall hear me company and the
    Bishop, don Jerome
So too this Muño Gustióz and Per Vermudóz
    shall come,
And Martin Antolínez from Burgos true and
    tried
And with Alvar Salvadórez, Alvar Alvarez
    beside,
And Martin Múñoz who was born in a season

of good grace,
So likewise Felez Múñoz a nephew of my race.
Mal Anda wise exceeding, along with me
    shall go
And the good Galínd Garcíaz of Aragon also.
With these knights a round hundred of the
    good men here ordain.
Let all men wear their tunics the harness to
    sustain
Let them assume the hauberks that white as
    sunlight glare,
And upon the hauberks ermines and mantles
    of the vair
Let them lace tight their armour, let not the
    arms be seen.
They shall bear beneath their mantles the
    swords both sweet and keen.
To the court in such a fashion to enter am I
    fain,
My rights there to demand them and to speak
    my meaning plain.
If there the Heirs of Carrión seek to
    dishonor me,
No whit then shall I fear them, though a
    hundred strong they be."
To him all gave their answer: "Such, lord, is
    our desire,"
Even as he had commanded they ordered
    their attire.

He who in happy hour was born would brook
    no more delay.
Upon his legs the hosen of fair cloth he drew
    straightway,
And shoes adorned most richly upon his feet
    has done;
he donned a shirt of linen fine as white as is
    the sun;
The sleeves are laced, moreover, with gold and
    silver braid.
The cuff fit close upon them for he bade them
    so be made.
Thereo'er a silken tunic most fairly wrought
    he drew.
The threads of gold shone brightly that were
    woven through and through.
A red fur gown gold-belted he cast his tunic
    o'er.
That gown alway he weareth, my lord Cid
    Campeador.
He hath of finest linen a cap upon his hair,
With the gold wrought, moreover, and
    fashioned with due care,
That the locks of the good Campeador might
    not be disarrayed.
And with a cord his mighty beard my lord the
    Cid doth braid.
All this he did desiring well his person to
    dispose.
O'er his attire a mantle of mighty worth he

throws.

Thereat might all men wonder that
thereabouts did stand.

Then with the chosen hundred whereto he
gave command

From San Serván forth issuing he got to horse
apace.

Under arms the Cid departed unto the
judgment-place.

Duly without the postern he descended from
his horse,

And prudently he entered the palace with his
force.

Midmost he went; his hundred girt him round
on every side.

When they had seen him enter, who was born
in happy tide,

Then the good King Alfonso upon his feet did
rise,

So also Count don Henry, and Count don
Remónd likewise.

And they arose, the others of the court, ye
well may know.

To him who in good hour was born great
honor did they show.

One man there was arose not – 'twas Crespo
de Grañón –

Nor any of the party of the Heirs of Carrión.

The King has ta'en my lord Cid's hand:

"Come sit thee, Campeador,
On the bench here beside me – thy gift to me
    of yore.
Thou art our better, though there be umbrage
    therefor that take."
Then he who won Valencia for gratitude he
    spake:
"Sit like a king and master on thy bench, for it
    is thine;
In this station will I tarry here with these men
    of mine."

Of what my lord Cid uttered was the King's
    heart glad and fain.
Upon a bench well carven the Cid his seat has
    ta'en;
The hundred men that guard him are seated
    round him there.
And all men in the Cortes upon my lord Cid
    stare,
And the long beard he weareth that is braided
    with a cord.
He seems by his apparel to be a splendid lord.
For shame the Heirs of Carrión his gaze they
    could not meet.

The good King don Alfonso then rose unto his
    feet:
"Hearken ye gentle companies, so God your
    hands sustain.

But two court have I holden in the space of all
    my reign.
In Burgos one, in Carrión the next did I array;
The third here in Toledo have I come to hold
    today,
For the Cid's love, whose birth-hour for a glad
    time is known,
That so he may have justice on the Heirs of
    Carrión.
Let all men know they did him a bitter injury
The Counts Remónd and Henry judges
    thereof shall be,
And all you counts, moreover, in the feud who
    bear no part.
In your minds turn it over, for ye are wise of
    heart.
See that ye render justice. All falseness I
    gainsay.
On one side and the other let us keep the
    peace this day.
Who breaks our peace, I swear it by the Saint
    Isidore
Shall be banished from my kingdom, nor have
    my favor more.
His side I will maintain it whose cause is right
    and fair.
Therefore let the Cid Campeador forthwith
    his suit declare.
Then shall we hear what Carrión's Heirs in
    answer shall depose."

My lord Cid kissed the King his hand. Then to
    his feet he rose:
"My sovereign and my master great thanks I
    give to thee
That thou this court hast summoned out of
    pure love for me.
Against the Heirs of Carrión this matter I
    reclaim.
They cast away my daughters. I had thereby
    no shame,
For thou gavest them in marriage. What deed
    to do today
Thou know'st well. From Valencia when they
    took my girls away,
I loved with heart and spirit the Heirs of
    Carrión,
And the two swords I gave them, Coláda and
    Tizón–
I won them in such manner as a good knight
    became–
That they might do you service and do honor
    to their fame.
When in the Wood of Corpes they left my
    girls forlorn,
They lost my love forever, for they made of me
    a scorn.
Since my sons-in-law they are not, let them
    give me either sword."
"All of the claim is righteous," so the judges
    gave accord.

Then said Count don García: "Of this let us
  debate."
Apart from the assizes went the Heirs of
  Carrión straight,
And all their following with them and the
  kindred of their name.
And swiftly they debated, and to their resolve
  they came:
"Now the Cid Campeador for us doth a great
  favor do,
Since for his girls' dishonor for no damage
  doth he sue.
With the King don Alfonso, we soon shall be
  at one.
The swords them let us give him, for so the
  suit is done;
They will hold the court no longer, when he
  has the swords once more.
From us no further justice for the Cid
  Campeador."
That parley being over, to court they get them
  now.

"Thy favor, King Alfonso, our overlord art
  thou.
And we cannot deny it, for he gave us the two
  brands.
And since that we return them he desires now
  and demands,
Into his hand to give them in thy presence are

we fain."

Then they brought forth Coláda and Tizón,
    the falchions twain,

Straightway they gave them over to the King
    their sovereign's hands.

The whole court shone glorious when they
    brought forth the brands.

The pommels and the hilt-bars are all of
    massy gold;

To the true henchmen of the court 'twas a
    marvel to behold.

The King my lord Cid summoned, to him the
    swords he gave.

His sovereign's hands he kisseth. He receiveth
    either glaive.

To the bench whence he had risen, he turned
    him back again,

And in his hands he held them, he looked
    upon the twain.

Changelings they could not give him; he knew
    the two aright,

And his heart laughed within him, he was
    filled with all delight.

"Now by my beard none ever plucked,"
    gripping it hard he spake,

For Dame Sol and Dame Elvíra high
    vengeance I will take."

By name his nephew Pero he has called out
    before;

And stretching forth his hand, to him the
    sword Tizón gave o'er.
"Take it nephew. The sword's master now is
    fairer of renown."
To good Martin Antolínez the man of Burgos
    town,
Stretching forth his hand Coláda into his care
    he gave;

"Thou Martin Antolínez, who art a vassal
    brave,
Take Coláda that I captured from a true
    knight without fail,
From him of Barcelona, from Remónd
    Berenguél.
That thou mayst guard it rightly, therefore I
    give it thee,
I know if aught befall thee, if occasion e'er
    should be,
Great fame and estimation with the sword
    shalt thou attain."
The lord Cid's hands he kissed them. He took
    the sword again.

My lord the Cid the Campeador unto his feet
    rose he;
"Now thanks to the Creator and my lord the
    King to thee.
With the swords Coláda and Tizón I am
    content indeed,

But I have a farther issue 'gainst Carrión Heirs
    to plead:

When with them from Valencia my daughters
    twain they bore,

Three thousand marks of silver and gold I
    gave them o'er.

When I did this, the winning of all their end
    they saw.

Let them restore the treasure. They are not
    my sons-in-law."

Now might you hearken Carrión's Heirs, what
    a complaint made they.

To them said the Count don Remónd: "Give
    answer, 'Yea' or 'Nay'!',

And then the Heirs of Carrión, they made
    their answer plain:

"Therefore to the Cid Campeador we gave his
    swords again

That he might demand naught further, for his
    suit is closed thereby."

Then straightway the Count don Remónd
    unto them made reply:

"This say we: With the pleasure of the
    Sovereign if it stands,

You shall give satisfaction in what the Cid
    demands."

The good King said: "The measure with my
    assent doth meet."

And now hath the Cid Campeador arisen to

his feet:

"Say of those goods I gave you, will ye give
    them me anew
Or render an accounting?"

Then Carrión's Heirs withdrew.
For the greatness of that treasure they could
    not as one consent,
And the two Heirs of Carrión the whole of it
    had spent.
They returned with their decision, and spake
    their pleasure thus:
"The Captor of Valencia, he presses sore on us.
Since lust for our possession so on him hand
    hath laid,
From our estates in Carrión the money shall
    be paid."

And then outspake the judges since the debt
    the Heirs avowed:
"If it be the Cid's desire, it is not disallowed.
So we ordain, for such wise with our pleasure
    doth it sort,
That ye repay it to him in this place before
    the court."

Out spake the King Alfonso when their words
    were at an end:
"The inward of this lawing we wholly
    comprehend,

That justice is demanded by the Cid
    Campeador.
Now of those marks three thousand, I have in
    hand tenscore;
They were given to me duly by the Heirs of
    Carrión twain.
Since so sore are they impoverished, I will
    give it them again.
To the Cid born in fair hour, let them pay the
    money back.
To pay their debt, that money I will not let
    them lack."

As for Ferránd Gonzálvez, what he said ye
    now shall hear:
"We have in our possession no minted goods
    and gear."

To him then the Count don Remónd answered
    to this intent:
"All of the gold and silver, the twain of you
    have spent.
Before the King Alfonso, our verdict we
    proclaim,
That ye pay in goods. The Campeador, let him
    accept the same."

Now saw the Heirs of Carrión what need must
    be their course.
Ye might have seen led thither full many a
    swift horse,

Many fat mules, moreover, and many a well-
    paced jade,

And every sort of armour, and many a fine
    blade.

My lord the Cid accepted even as the court
    assessed,

Beyond the tenscore marks whereof Alfonso
    stood possessed,

To him who in good hour was born the Heirs
    have paid the price.

On others' goods they borrow, for their own
    will not suffice

Know well for fools men took them, from that
    suit when 'scaped the twain.

CXXXVIII.

All of those great possessions my lord the Cid
    has ta'en.

The men keep all that treasure, and they will
    ward it well.

When this was done, a-pondering on other
    things they fell:

Lord King, for love of charity, a further favor
    yet,

Of my complaints the chiefest, I cannot now
    forget.

Let the whole court now hear me, and have
    pity on my woe:

As for these Heirs of Carrión, the which have
    shamed me so,

I brook not that unchallenged they may go
    hence away.

CXXXIX.

"In what thing I affronted you, ye Heirs of
    Carrión say,
In what fashion whatsoever, in earnest or in
    sport.
Let me make amends according to the
    judgment of the court.
Why did ye tear in tatters the fabric of my
    heart?
With great honor from Valencia what time ye
    did depart,
I gave to you my daughters, and besides great
    wealth and gear.
Now say, ye dogs and traitors, since ye did not
    hold them dear,
Why took ye from Valencia what was their
    dower of right,
And wherefore with the girth and spur the
    ladies did ye smite?
Alone in Corpes Forest ye cast the twain away,
Unto the savage creatures and the wood-fowl
    for a prey.
In all ye did unto them, like vile men did ye
    show.
Let the Court judge; satisfaction shall I get
    therefor or no?"

CXL.

And lo! Count don García has risen up amain:

"Let us now have thy favor, best of all kings in
Spain.

Of the courts proclaimed is now the Cid well
versed in the affairs.

Since he let it wax so mighty, 'tis a long beard
he wears.

Some he affrights and others are for fear in
sorry case.

But as for them of Carrión, theirs is a lofty
race,

His daughters e'en as lemans to love becomes
them not.

Who to them for lawful consorts those ladies
would allot?

When they cast them off, then did they as
might the right befit.

All things he says soever we value not a whit."

And thereupon the Campeador his beard in
hand gripped he:

"To God who ruleth Heaven and the whole
Earth glory be.

Since tenderly I kept it, is my beard grown so
long.

Count, say what is the reason, that thou dost
my beard this wrong,

That since its first growth ever has been so
gently reared.

No man born of woman has ever plucked that
    beard.
Nor has son of Moor or Christian e'er torn
    that beard of mine,
As once in Cabra Castle I did, oh Count, to
    thine,
When at one time on Cabra and thy beard my
    hand I set.
Not a lad but for the plucking his pinch
    thereof could get.
Nor is it yet grown even what portion I did
    tear.
Here hidden in my wallet those tokens yet I
    bear."

CXLI.

Now had Ferránd Gonzálvez risen to his feet
    that tide.
What thing ye now shall hearken that there so
    loud he cried:

"Cid, do thou now give over the suit which
    thou hast made,
For the whole of thy possession into thine
    hands is paid.
Look that thou make not greater the feud
    twixt us and thee,
For the two Counts of Carrión by lineage
    are we.
Of kings' and emperors' daughters are we fit
    to win the hands;

To wed the girls of little chiefs scarce with
    our lineage stands.
When thy daughters we abandoned we did but
    what was right.
Not worse therefor but better, are we then in
    our own sight."

CXLII.

To Per Vermudóz Roy Diaz my lord the Cid
    looked now:
"Speak then, good Pero Mudo, though a silent
    man art thou.
The ladies are my daughters, thy cousins
    twain are they.
Into thy teeth they cast it, when such a thing
    they say.
Thou shalt not do this battle, if I the answer
    make.

CXLIII.

And thereupon Per Vermudóz began the tale
    and spake.
No words he utters clearly, for 'tis a tongue-
    halt man.
Natheless no rest he gave them, be it known,
    when he began:

"To thee, Cid, now I tell it, for such thy
    customs be,
That in Court, Pero Mudo, ever thou callest
    me.

And verily thou knowest that I can do no
    more.
As for what I must accomplish, there shall be
    no lack therefore.

"What thing thou saidest soever, Ferrándo,
    was a lie.
Through the Campeador thy glory was risen
    yet more high.
I can relate unto thee thine every trick and
    sleight.
Minds't thou, near high Valencia, what time
    we fought the fight?
Thou didst of the true Campeador for the
    first onslaught pray.
And there a Moor thou sawest, whom thou
    wentest forth to slay.
Or e'er thou camest to him, before him didst
    thou flee.
If aid I had not borne thee, he had roughly
    handled thee.
But I rushed on beyond thee, and with the
    Moor did close,
And I made that Moor flee backward at the
    foremost of my blows.
To thee I gave his charger, and kept the thing
    concealed.
Until this day that cowardice I never have
    revealed.
Before the Cid and all men thine own praises

didst thou sing,
How thou slewest the Morisco, and didst a
    gallant thing.
And they believed it of thee, knowing not the
    truth at all.
Of thy person art thou handsome, but thy
    courage it is small,
Tongue without hands, the manhood to speak
    where gottest thou?

CXLIV.

"Do thou say on, Ferrándo. That my words are
    truth avow:
That matter of the lion in Valencia dost thou
    keep
In mind still, when he burst his bonds while
    the Cid lay asleep?
Ferrándo, then what didst thou, when thy
    terror overbore?
Thou didst thrust thyself behind the bench of
    the Cid Campeador.
Thou didst hide, Ferrándo, wherefore cheap
    today thy worth is found,
But we to guard our master his pallet
    gathered round,
Till he who won Valencia out of his sleep did
    wake.
He rose up from the pallet, at the lion did he
    make.
His head the lion bended, for the Cid the

beast did wait.

By the neck he let himself be ta'en. In the cage
he thrust him straight.

When came once more the Campeador, there
he saw his vassals stand.

He asked about his sons-in-law, but neither
found at hand.

For a wicked man and traitor thy person I
arraign.

In fight before Alfonso that same I will
maintain,

For Dame Sol and Dame Elvíra, for the Cid's
daughters' sake.

Thou didst cast away the ladies thine honor
cheap to make.

Ye are men to all appearance, tender women
are those two;

Yet in every way whatever they are worthier
than you.

If, when we join the combat, God shall like
well in his heart,

Thyself shalt thou confess it, like a traitor as
thou art.

Whatever I have uttered shall then be known
for true."

And thereupon was ending of speech between
these two.

CXLV.

And Dídago Gonzálvez what he uttered ye

shall hear:

"We twain are Counts by lineage of blood of
the most clear.

Such marriages in no way we twain would
undertake,

With my lord Cid don Rodrigo alliance for to
make.

We do not yet repent us that we put his
daughters by:

So long as life endureth, may they sigh many
a sigh.

A sore reproach upon them what we did will
still remain.

The same with utmost valor in the fight will I
maintain:

When we cast away the women we made our
honor good."

CXLVI.

Then Martin Antolínez upon his feet he
stood:

Thou wretch, do thou keep silence. Mouth
that truth knoweth not!

The matter of the lion hast thou so soon
forgot

Out through the door thou fleddest lurking
in the court outside,

Behind the wine-press timber in that hour
didst thou hide.

That mantle and that tunic were worn no

more by thee.
In fight I will maintain it. No other can it be.
Since the lord Cid his daughters forth in such
plight ye threw,
They are in every fashion far worthier shall
you.
At the ending of the combat then thine own
mouth shall avow
That lies are all thine utterance, and a traitor
knave art thou."

CXLVII.
Between those two the parley has come unto
an end.
Now did Ansuór Gonzálvez into the palace
wend.
Was an ermine cloak about him, and his tunic
trailed behind.
His countenance was ruddy, for but lately had
he dined.
In what he had to utter small discretion did
he show:

CXLVIII.
"How now ye noble gentlemen, was ever such
a woe?
With Bivár's lord Cid such honor who would
have thought to find?
On the Ovirna water his millstones let him
grind,
And take his wonted toll-corn. Would any man

have thought
That with the Heirs of Carrión alliances he
    sought?"

CXLIX.
And then did Muño Gustióz rise to his feet
    forthright:
"Thou wretch, do thou keep silent! Thou
    wicked traitor wight!
Before to prayers thou goest, certain thou art
    to dine.
Whoe'er in peace thou kissest, sickens at that
    belch of thine.
Whether to friend or master thou speakest
    perjury,
False unto all, and falsest to the God who
    fashioned thee!
And never in thy friendship will I have any
    part,
And I will make thee say it that what I say
    thou art."

Said now the King Alfonso: "Let the suit quiet
    lie.
Who have challenged shall do battle, so help
    me the Most High."

Soon as the suit was finished to the court two
    horsemen came,
And Inigo Ximénez and Ojárra men them
    name;

For Navarra's Heir-apparent, proxy-suitor was
    the one,
The other was the suitor for the Heir of
    Aragon.
And there the twain together have kissed
    Alfonso's hand,
The Cid Campeador his daughters in marriage
    they demand,
Of the realms Navarre and Aragon the lady-
    queens to be.
May he send them with his blessing and with
    all courtesy.
Thereat the whole court listened, and
    stillness fell them o'er.
Upon his feet rose straightway my lord Cid
    Campeador:
"A boon, Oh King Alfonso, my sovran lord
    thou art.
For this to the Creator very thankful is my
    heart,
Since both Navarre and Aragon have made
    request so high.
Thou didst give to wed my daughters before.
    It was not I.
Here then behold my daughters, the twain are
    in thine hand.
With them I will do nothing, except at thy
    command."
The King rose up. For silence in the court the
    word he gave:

"I beg it of thee, Campeador, the true Cid and
      the brave,
That hereto thou yield agreement. I will grant
      the thing this day:
And it shall be consented in open court
      straightway,
For so will grow thy glory and shine honor
      and thy lands."
Now is the Cid arisen. He kissed Alfonso's
      hands:
"To whatever thing shall please thee, I give
      consent, my lord."
Then said the King: "God grant thee an
      excellent reward!
To Inigo Ximénez and Ojárra, to you two,
I yield my full permission for this marriage
      unto you,
That Dame Sol and Dame Elvíra, who the Cid's
      daughters are,
Wed, one the Heir of Aragon, and the other of
      Navarre.
May he yield his girls with blessings in an
      honorable way."

Then Inigo Ximénez and Ojárra, up rose they,
And the hands of Don Alfonso in that hour
      kissed again.
The hands of the Cid Campeador thereafter
      kissed the twain,
And there their faith they plighted, and

solemn oaths they swore,
That they would fulfill entirely what they
    promised or yet more.
Because of this were many in the court
    exceeding glad;
But the two Heirs of Carrión, therein no joy
    they had.

Minaya Alvar Fañez upon his feet rose he:
"As from my King and Master I beg a boon of
    thee,
And let it not be grievous to the Cid
    Campeador.
I have through these assizes kept my peace
    heretofore,
But now to utter somewhat for mine own part
    fain am I."
Said the King: "Now all my spirit, it is well
    pleased thereby.
Say on! Say on, Minaya, what to thy heart is
    dear."

"You in the court, I beg you to my word to
    lend an ear.
'Gainst Carrión's Heirs needs must I now a
    charge most mighty bring:
I gave to them my cousins by Alfonso's hand,
    the King.
With blessings and with honor they took
    them in their care.

The Cid Campeador he gave them most rich
    possessions there.
They cast away those ladies, for all that we
    were loth.
For wicked men and traitors I make challenge
    of you both.
From the great sons of Gomez does your
    lineage come down,
Whence many counts have issued of valor and
    renown,
But this day all to certainly their cunning do
    we learn.
For this to the Creator, now thanks do I
    return,
That of Navarre and Aragon the Heirs in
    marriage sue
For Dame Sol and Elvíra that are my cousins
    two.
Erst for true wives ye had them, who now
    their hands shall kiss
And call them Dame, though sorely ye take
    the thing amiss.
Praise to our God in Heaven and our lord the
    King therefor.
So greatly grows the honor of the Cid my
    Campeador.
In every way soever ye are even as I say.
Is there any in the presence to reply or say me
    nay?
Lo! I am Alvar Fañez, against the most of

might!"

And thereupon did Gomez Peláez stand
    upright:
"Say of what worth, Minaya, is this ye speak so
    free?
For here in the assizes are men enough for
    thee.
Who otherwise would have it, it would ruin
    him indeed.
If it be perchance God's pleasure that our
    quarrel well should speed,
Then well shalt thou see whether or right or
    wrong ye were."
Said the King: "The suit is over. No further
    charge prefer.
Tomorrow is the combat; at the rising of the
    sun
By the three who challenged with thee in the
    court it shall be done."

Thereon the Heirs of Carrión have spoken
    presently:
"Lord King, a season grant us for tomorn it
    cannot be.
We have given to the Campeador our arms and
    many a steed,
First to our land of Carrión to go we have sore
    need."
And then the King had spoken to the

Campeador again:

"Where thou shalt bid, this combat, let it be
    underta'en.

"My lord, I will not do it," my lord the Cid said
    he,

"More than the lands of Carrión Valencia
    liketh me."

To him the King gave answer:

"Yea, Cid! Without a doubt.

Give unto me your cavaliers all duly armed
    about.

Let them go in my keeping. Their safety I
    assure

As a lord to a good vassal; I make thee here
    secure

That they take no harm from any count or
    lesser baronet.

Here now in the assizes, a term for them I set,

That in the fields of Carrión at the end of
    three weeks' space

There duly in my presence the combat shall
    take place.

Who at the set time comes not, his suit is lost
    thereby,

From that time he is vanquished; for a traitor
    let him fly."

The two heirs of Carrión, by that decree they
    stand.

And thereupon my lord the Cid has kissed the

King his hand;

"To thy hand are they delivered my cavaliers
    all three;
As to my King and Master I commend them
    unto thee.
They are ready now their duty to the full to
    undertake.
With honor to Valencia send them me for God
    his sake."
"So it be God's desire," answered the King and
    said.
The Cid the Campeador did off the helmet
    from his head,
Likewise the cap of linen as white as is the
    sun.
He freed his beard, the cord thereof he has
    forthwith undone.
Those in the court upon him, their full they
    could not gaze.
To the Counts Remónd and Henry forthwith
    he went his way.
And them closely he embraces and doth
    heartily require
To take of his possession all that suits with
    their desire.
These twain and many others who were
    persons of good will
He earnestly requested to take unto their fill
Some took his gifts, but others would not

accept a thing.

The two hundred marks, he gave them once
more unto the King.

Whatever was his pleasure he has taken of the
rest:

"King, for love of the Creator one thing let me
request.

Sire, with thy will I kiss thine hand. Since so
these deeds are done,

And would fain unto Valencia which with
great pain I won."

*Then the Cid commanded to give sumpter-beasts
unto the embassadors*

*of the Heirs of Navarre and Aragon, and, moreover,
to let them*

*have whatever else they required. And he sent them
forth.*

*The King don Alfonso with all the nobles of his court
got on horseback*

*in order to ride out with the Cid who was about to
leave the town.*

*When they came to Zocodover, the Cid being on his
charger Baviéca, the King said to him:*

*"In faith, don Rodrigo, thou must now put spur to
that charger of*

which I have heard most fair report."

*The Cid smiled and said: "Sire, in thy court, are
many, gentle and*

simple, who would gladly do such a thing. Bid them
*   make sport with their steeds."*

The King replied to him: "Cid, I am pleased with
*   thine answer.*
Nevertheless I desire thee, for the love thou bearest
*   me, to put that steed through his best paces."*[2]

CL.
The Cid then put spur to the charger and
    made him gallop
so fast that all were astonished at the career
    he ran.

The King with hand uplifted signed the cross
    upon his face.
"By San Isidro of León, I swear it by his grace
Is no nobleman so mighty our whole country
    o'er."
My lord Cid on the charger came then the
    King before,
And of his lord Alfonso there has he kissed
    the hand.

"To start fleet Baviéca thou gavest me
    command.
Today no Moor nor Christian has a horse so
    strong and swift.
Sire, unto thee I give him. Say thou wilt
    accept the gift."

---

2.   Supplied like the former prose passage from the *Chronicle of the*
     Twenty Kings.

Then said the King:

"No pleasure would I have therein indeed.

If I took him, then less glorious were the
    master of the steed.

But a horse like this befitteth too well a man
    like thee,

Swift to chase the Moors ye routed in the
    battle, when they flee.

Who that war-horse taketh from thee, God
    succor not again,

For by thee and by the charger to great honor
    we attain."

Their leave then have they taken. He left the
    Court forthright.

The Campeador most wisely counselled them
    who were to fight:

"Ha, Martin Antolínez! Per Vermudóz thou,
    too,

So likewise Muño Gustióz, my tried man and
    true.

Be resolute in combat like the gentlemen
    ye be.

See that of you good tidings in Valencia come
    to me."

Said Martin Antolínez: "Oh sire, what sayest
    thou?

For we must bear the burden we accepted
    even now.

Thou shalt hear naught of the vanquished,

though haply of the slain."
He who in happy hour was born, thereof was
    glad and fain.
Of all his leave he taketh that for his friends
    are known.
Went my lord Cid to Valencia, and the King to
    Carrión.

But now the three weeks' respite of the term
    is past and o'er.
Lo! at the time appointed, they who serve the
    Campeador,
The debt their lord laid on them they were
    very fain to pay.
In safe-keeping of Alfonso, King of León, were
    they.
There for the Heirs of Carrión for two days'
    space they stayed.
With horses and caparisons, came the Heirs
    there well arrayed.
And in close compact with them have agreed
    their kinsmen all,
On the Campeador his henchmen, if in secret
    they might fall,
To slay them in the meadows, because their
    lords were silent.
They did not undertake it, though foul was
    their intent,
For of Alfonso of León they stood in mighty
    dread.

Watch o'er their arms they kept that night.
    And prayers to God they said.

At last has night passed over, and breaketh
    now the dawn,
And many worthy nobles there to the place
    have drawn,
For to behold that combat, wherefore their
    mirth was high.
Moreover King Alfonso above all men is by,
Since he desireth justice and that no wrong
    should be done.
The men of the good Campeador, they get
    their armour on.
All three are in agreement for one lord's men
    are they.
The Heirs of Carrión elsewhere have armed
    them for the fray.
The Count García Ordoñez sate with them in
    counsel there.
What suit they planned unto the King Alfonso
    they declare,
That neither should Coláda nor Tizón share
    in that war,
That in fight they might not wield them, who
    served the Campeador
That the brands were given over, they deemed
    a bitter ill;
Unto the King they told it. He would not do
    their will:

"When we held the court exception unto no
    sword did ye take;
But if ye have good weapons, your fortune
    they will make.
For them who serve the Campeador the
    swords e'en so will do.
Up, Carrión's Heirs, to battle now get you
    forth, ye two!
Like noblemen this combat, ye ought duly to
    achieve,
For the Campeador his henchmen naught
    undone therein will leave.
If forth, ye come victorious, then great shall
    be your fame;
But if that ye are vanquished, impute to us no
    blame.
All know ye sought it."
Carrión's Heirs were filled with grief
    each one.
And greatly they repented the thing that they
    had done.
Were it undone fain were they to give all
    Carrión's fee.

The henchmen of the Campeador are fully
    armed all three.
Now was the King Alfonso come forth to view
    them o'er.
Then spake to him the henchmen that served
    the Campeador:

"We kiss thy hands as vassals to their lord and
    master may,
'Twixt our party and their party thou shalt be
    judge this day.
For our succor unto justice but not to evil
    stand.
Here Carrión's Heirs of henchmen have
    gathered them a band.
What, or what not, we know not, that in secret
    they intend;
But our lord in thine hand left us our safety
    to defend.
For the love of the Creator justly maintain our
    part."
Said then the King in answer: "With all my
    soul and heart."

They brought for them the chargers of
    splendid strength and speed.
They signed the cross upon the selles. They
    leaped upon the steed.
The bucklers with fair bosses about their
    necks are cast.
And the keen pointed lances, in the hand they
    grip them fast.
Each lance for each man of the three doth its
    own pennon bear.
And many worthy nobles have gathered round
    them there.
To the field where were the boundaries,

accordingly they went.
The three men of the Campeador were all of
    one intent,
That mightily his foeman to smite each one
    should ride.
Lo! were the Heirs of Carrión upon the other
    side,
With stores of men, for many of their kin
    were with the two.
The King has given them judges, justice and
    naught else to do,
That yea or nay they should not any
    disputation make.
To them where in the field they sate the King
    Alfonso spake:
"Hearken, ye Heirs of Carrión, what thing to
    you I say:
In Toledo ye contrived it, but ye did not wish
    this fray.
Of my lord Cid the Campeador I brought
    these knights all three
To Carrión's land, that under my safe-conduct
    they might be.
Wait justice. Unto evil no wise turn your
    intent.
Whoso desireth evil with force will I prevent;
Such a thing throughout my kingdom he shall
    bitterly bemoan."
How downcast were the spirits of the Heirs of
    Carrión!

Now with the King the judges have marked
    the boundaries out.
They have cleared all the meadow of people
    roundabout.
And unto the six champions the boundaries
    have they shown–
Whoever went beyond them should be held
    for overthrown.
The folk that round were gathered now all the
    space left clear;
To approach they were forbidden within six
    lengths of a spear.
'Gainst the sun no man they stationed, but by
    lot gave each his place.
Forth between them came the judges, and the
    foes are face to face.
Of my lord Cid the henchmen toward the
    Heirs of Carrión bore,
And Carrión's Heirs against them who served
    the Campeador.
The glance of every champion fixes on his
    man forthright;
Before their breasts the bucklers with their
    hands have they gripped tight,
The lances with the pennons now have they
    pointed low,
And each bends down his countenance over
    the saddlebow;
Thereon the battle-chargers with the sharp
    spurs smote they,

And fain the earth had shaken where the
    steeds sprang away.
The glance of every champion fixes on his
    man forthright.
Three against three together now have they
    joined the fight.
Whoso stood round for certain deemed that
    they dead would fall.
Per Vermudóz the challenge who delivered
    first of all,
Against Ferránd Gonzálvez there face to face
    he sped.
They smote each other's bucklers withouten
    any dread.
There has Ferránd Gonzálvez pierced don
    Pero's target through.
Well his lance-shaft in two places he shattered
    it in two.
Unto the flesh it came not, for there glanced
    off the steel.
Per Vermudóz sat firmly, therefore he did not
    reel.
For every stroke was dealt him, the buffet
    back he gave,
He broke the boss of the buckler, the shield
    aside he drave.
He clove through guard and armour, naught
    availed the man his gear.
Nigh the heart into the bosom he thrust the
    battle-spear.

Three mail-folds had Ferrándo, and the third
  was of avail.
Two were burst through, yet firmly held the
  third fold of mail.
Ferrándo's shirt and tunic, with the unpierced
  iron mesh,
A handsbreadth by Per Vermudóz were thrust
  into the flesh.
And forth from his mouth straightway a
  stream of blood did spout.
His saddle-girths were broken; not one of
  them held out.
O'er the tail of the charger he hurled him to
  the ground.
That his death stroke he had gotten thought
  all the folk around.
He left the war-spear in him, set hand his
  sword unto.
When Ferránd Gonzálvez saw it, then well
  Tizón he knew.
He shouted, "I am vanquished," rather than
  the buffet bear.
Per Vermudóz, the judges so decreeing, left
  him there.

CLI.
With Dídago Gonzálvez now doth don Martin
  close
The spears. They broke the lances so furious
  were the blows.

Martin Antolínez on sword his hand he laid.

The whole field shone, so brilliant and
    flawless was the blade.

He smote a buffet. Sidewise it caught him fair
    and right.

Aside the upper helmet the glancing stroke
    did smite.

It clove the helmet laces. Through the mail-
    hood did it fall,

Unto the coif, hard slashing through coif and
    helm and all,

And scraped the hair upon his brow. Clear to
    the flesh it sped.

Of the helm a half fell earthward and half
    crowned yet his head.

When the glorious Coláda such a war-stroke
    had let drive,

Well knew Dídago Gonzálvez that he could
    not 'scape alive.

He turned the charger's bridle rein, and right
    about he wheeled.

A blade in hand he carried that he did not
    seek to wield.

From Martin Antolínez welcome with the
    sword he got.

With the flat Martin struck him. With the
    edge he smote him not.

Thereon that Heir of Carrión, a mighty yell he
    gave:

"Help me, Oh God most glorious, defend me

from that glaive."
Wheeling his horse, in terror he fled before
    the blade.
The steed bore him past the boundary. On the
    field don Martin stayed.
Then said the King: "Now hither come unto
    my meinie.
Such a deed thou hast accomplished as has
    won this fight for thee."
That a true word he had spoken so every
    judge deemed well.

CLII.

The twain had won. Now let us of Muño
    Gustióz tell,
How with Ansuór Gonzálvez of himself
    account he gave.
Against each other's bucklers the mighty
    strokes they drave.
Was Ansuór Gonzálvez a gallant man of
    might.
Against don Muño Gustióz on the buckler did
    he smite,
And piercing through the buckler, right
    through the cuirass broke.
Empty went the lance; his body was
    unwounded by the stroke.
That blow struck, Muño Gustióz has let his
    buffet fly.
Through the boss in the middle was the

buckle burst thereby.
Away he could not ward it. Through his
    cuirass did it dart.
Through one side was it driven though not
    nigh unto the heart.
Through the flesh of his body he thrust the
    pennoned spear,
On the far side he thrust it a full fathom clear.
He gave one wrench. Out of the selle that
    cavalier he threw.
Down to the earth he cast him, when forth
    the lance he drew.
And shaft and lance and pennon all crimson
    came they out.
All thought that he was wounded to the death
    without a doubt.
The lance he has recovered, he stood the foe
    above.
Said Gonzálvo Ansuórez: "Smite him not for
    God his love.
Now is won out the combat for all this game is
    done."
"We have heard defeat conceded," said the
    judges every one.

The good King don Alfonso bade them clear
    the field straightway.
For himself he took the armour upon it yet
    that lay.
In honor have departed they who serve the

Campeador.
Glory be to the Creator, they have conquered
   in the war.
Throughout the lands of Carrión was sorrow
   at the height.

The King my lord Cid's henchmen has sent
   away by night,
That they should not be frightened or
   ambushed on the way,
Like men of prudent spirit they journeyed
   night and day.
Ho! in Valencia with the Cid the Campeador
   they stand.
On Carrión's Heirs of knavery the three have
   put the brand,
And paid the debt the lord Cid set upon them
   furthermore.
On that account right merry was the Cid
   Campeador.
Upon the heirs of Carrión is come a mighty
   smirch.
Who flouts a noble lady and leaves her in the
   lurch,
May such a thing befall him, or worse fortune
   let him find.
Of Carrión's Heirs the dealings let us leave
   them now behind.
For what has been vouchsafed them now were
   they all forlorn.

Of this man let us make mention who in
    happy hour was born.
And great are the rejoicings through Valencia
    the town,
Because the Campeador his men had won such
    great renown.
His beard their lord Roy Diaz hard in his hand
    has ta'en:
"Thanks to the King of Heaven, well are
    'venged my daughters twain.
Now may they hold their Carrión lands. Their
    shame is wiped away.
I will wed them in great honor, let it grieve
    whom it may."

They of Navarre and Aragon were busied now
    to treat,
And with Alfonso of León in conference they
    meet.
Dame Sol and Dame Elvíra in due course
    wedded are.
Great were their former matches, but these
    are nobler far.
He gave with greater honor than before the
    twain to wed;
He who in happy hour was born still doth his
    glory spread,
Since o'er Navarre and Aragon as queens his
    daughters reign;
Today are they kinswomen unto the kings of

Spain.

From him came all that honor who in good
hour had birth.

The Cid who ruled Valencia has departed from
the earth

At Pentecost. His mercy may Christ to him
extend.

To us all, just men or sinners, may He yet
stand our friend.

Lo! the deeds of the Cid Campeador! Here
takes the book an end.